TABLE OF CONTENTS

	Page
Introduction	v
Chapter	
I.—On the Determination of Truth	17
II.—The Sphere of Lust	38
III.—The Second, or Relational Sphere	61
IV.—Communication	76
V.—Philosophy of Progression	99
VI.—Mediumship	115
VII.—Mediumship—Spiritual Healing	130
VIII.—Condition of the Spirit in the Spirit-World	146
IX.—Organization—Individualization	160
X.—What Constitutes the Spirit	171
XI.—Lust	187
XII.—Marriage—Free Love	206

INTRODUCTION

The relations of man to his God have occupied the first minds of every age, but without rendering those relations so understandable to the mass of mankind as to be admitted as true. It has been evident to many, although not to all, that some minds so engaged have been inspired to write beyond the current knowledge of their day, indeed to foretell truths which could only be recognized as such after centuries of progression.

The natural propensity of the human mind in the exercise of its ingenuity has been constantly developing in the endeavor to theorize upon the writings of these inspired authors, so as to present an entire system for the consideration of man. Each of these systems so proposed has passed away, from the fact that it carried with it the elements of its own destruction, itself not arising purely from the absolute, and therefore subject to the analysis of progressed mind, and by such analysis found wanting. Those theories which might have seemed compatible with the ability to adjudge truth in the middle ages, were not truths to the more progressed minds of later times; so that truth, except to absolute consciousness, may be considered, when subject to the test of human comprehension, as not absolute even to such comprehension, except in degree, and that varying with the continued progression of the recipient. Thus the best minds at this time willingly admit that the writer of Job was inspired—that he wrote truths beyond the comprehension of more than a thousand years beyond his time. One instance of this may be thus stated:

To Galileo and Copernicus we have attributed the discovery of the fact that the world is round; and yet the writer of the Book of Job, who wrote a thousand years before them, tells us that the earth is round, that its north is frigid, that the waters are divided by the dry land, where the day becomes night, and the night becomes day—clearly indicating that the continents are twelve hours apart, and that the earth must revolve to enable the relative position of its parts to the sun to give the phenomena now so well understood.

Plato was an inspired man. He wrote on the soul, far in advance of his day; and it is only a progressed mind at this time that can read and comprehend his views. With Plato, all admit that his normal progression might have been equal to the observance of the results of his inspiration. But the writer of the Book of Job could never have seen an ocean. He could not have known of the existence of another continent, and the sciences collateral to his text could not have rendered him the didactic aid which would have been necessary to have made him cognizant, in his normal condition, of the truths he uttered; and, therefore, it is at least possible, if not probable, that these truths were directly the result of inspiration, as much beyond his own comprehension as beyond the comprehension of others. Indeed, even at the present day, thousands of students of theology have read Job without perceiving that he had fore-run Galileo and Copernicus in their supposed discoveries.

It is not to be wondered at, then, that modern Spiritualism and its truths, if credited to the source from which they are supposed to be derived, should be found to present truths not understood as such by every mind; and, notwithstanding its million converts, it seems to have embraced but few minds capable of presenting in a didactic form these truths. The various writers on the subject have rather spoken of its curiosities than its use; and we know of no book capable of instructing and satisfying even a progressed mind on either the precise use or exact advantages arising from a full belief in Spiritualism.

This task has been most fearlessly performed by Joel Tiffany, Esq. He brought to the work a vigorous and original mind. A long course of legal practice had peculiarly adapted him to the task, particularly as an investigator of truth. His own progression was such as to enable him to advantage by his former practice, while his mediative power gave him intuitive advantage seldom combined in the same individual. His course of lectures seems to be suited to the precise wants of the day. It is true that they are not calculated for the use of the novice, but they are the only source we know of at this time by which those who have passed through the curiosity-phase of the subject of Spiritualism are enabled to review their observations and apply them usefully to their own progression. All those properties of the mind known as *adjective* in common parlance, requiring the assistance of the observation of others to render them substantive, are clearly defined by Mr. Tiffany.

His analysis of mind, when properly understood, enables all the truths he has set forth to be read understandingly; in other words he gives the *modus* by which we may determine truths at least equal to the progressed condition of man at this time to comprehend.

The Sphere of Lust, that greatest bar to man's progression, both in its analysis and synthesis, is placed within his comprehension, and hence his power of avoidance is materially increased. The fabled terrors of Hades, Sheol, Tartarus, and Gehenna are defined so as to be comprehended by an ordinary individual, while the relational sphere of man is so treated as to enable each reader to define his own position, and those below him, sufficiently well to assist in his aspirations for higher exercise.

Communication and Progression are fearlessly treated, and the master-mind is observable in all the collateral incidents of thought consequent upon their investigation.

Mediumship is rendered understandable to all, and those phases which have been unproductive of good results to minds not elevated beyond the consideration consequent upon the morbid appetites of the curious, are fairly depicted so as to enable the investigator to avoid their recurrence, and to progress beyond their painful influences.

Mr. Tiffany has judiciously failed to cater to the tastes of those who but magnify Kings to conceive of Gods. He has presented the Deity, or the consideration of the Deity, to the minds of his audience, in such a manner as to call forth the highest feelings of the soul for the comprehension of the highest truth.

The condition of the Spirit in the Spirit-world, as portrayed by him, is freed from the melo-dramatic condition in which it has been painted by the fashionable and various theologians of the day. The character of those Spirits is shown to be in accordance with the great law of God—Progression.

While we freely admit the usefulness and beauty of many works written on abstract phases of Spiritualism, we can not but perceive a want of continuity in their didactic character; and from the point where the mind admits a future state of existence to the supposed character of that existence and the proper preparation of the Spirit while in the form for entering upon such a condition, we can not but observe that no work preceding these Lectures by Mr. Tiffany has met the demand. A careful reading of these Lectures, we are confident, will elevate and instruct every Spiritualist. It will enable him to review his intuitions, and to find their true value. It will chasten his confidence in communications which are not self-evident as truths, and improve his power to comprehend these truths.

We ask the reader to peruse the following pages no more rapidly than he can clearly comprehend them. Every proposition is worthy his best thought and highest power of study; and if he follows them with the same pure aspiration that seems to imbue their author, he will rise from their consideration a wiser and a better man.

PHENIX.

CHAPTER I.
ON THE DETERMINATION OF TRUTH.

In commencing the investigation of Spiritualism, it becomes necessary in the outset that we find some point from which to start, or to commence our examination; for, in the inquiry after truth, we must find some standard by which we can determine truth—for unless we have that to which we can appeal to determine infallibly what is truth, however much we may investigate, we shall always be uncertain as to the accuracy of our conclusions.

Man, as a conscious being, endowed with the faculty of perceiving being and existence, and also being susceptible to the influence of that which he perceives, himself becomes the center of all his investigations in the universe; and if there is any standard by which to try truth, he must find that standard within his own consciousness. Outside of man's consciousness there is no standard to him of truth.

I will illustrate briefly what I mean, that you may perceive how I wish to direct you in the investigation of the question, What is Truth? and how shall it be determined? The science of mathematics is said to be certain and demonstrative. And why is the science of mathematics any more demonstrable than is any other science? Why is it that the truth which it affirms can be any more positively demonstrated than any other truth? Is it because number and quantity are more fixed and certain than are qualities and attributes of being and existence? Why is it that the affirmations of mathematics are more demonstrable than the truths of any other science? I answer, that it is simply owing to the mode of proceeding in our investigations. If we will adopt the same process that we do in mathematics, we can have the same certainty upon all other questions that come within the sphere of man's perceptions and affections. The mathematician comes down into his own consciousness, and finds certain conscious affirmations pertaining to number and quantity. He puts them down as truths not to be disregarded, and calls them self-evident truths or axioms. They are such affirmations of the consciousness as everybody must, per force, admit to be true; and when he has obtained the affirmations of his consciousness pertaining to number and quantity, he puts them down as truths not to be disregarded. They are always true everywhere, and under all circumstances, where number and quantity are to be investigated. He assumes nothing to be true which conflicts with these conscious affirmations of the soul. "Things equal to the same thing are equal to one another" must be received as true throughout the wide universe, so far as the mathematician investigates; and he allows nothing to controvert that self-evident truth; and so of all other affirmations. He allows nothing, in his investigations, to conflict at all; and whatever does conflict, he affirms to be false. Then, before he takes another step, he is very careful to fix upon accurate definitions, so that we may know precisely what he means—may understand exactly the scope of what he says. For instance, speaking of geometry, he will say that it pertains to the measurement of extent, and extent has three dimensions—length, breadth, and thickness. He next goes on to give definitions of that which is necessary to bound space—tells you what is a straight line, what a curved line, what is a plain surface, what is a curved surface, etc. After having ascertained the affirmations of the consciousness of the soul, in respect to number and quantity, and having fixed accurately upon the definition of all terms to be used, he then commences by demonstration, and will not go one step faster than demonstration attends him—does not launch at all into conjecture. He makes the relation between premises and conclusion inevitable; and if there be not an inevitable relation, he does not establish his proposition mathematically.

Now, what is true in respect to mathematics, is true in respect to every other subject that may come before the mind. There are conscious affirmations of the soul lying at the basis of all investigation; and in these conscious affirmations of the soul is to be found the standard by which to try the truth of whatever plane or sphere of thought. The first point to be taken is to ascertain what are the affirmations of the soul upon these points to be investigated. Our next step is to fix upon certain definitions, so that we can always understand precisely what we mean in our use of terms. Then we must see next that the relation between premises and conclusion be always inevitable. There must never be left any opportunity for the premises to be true and the conclusion false. Then we shall always be certain of having the truth.

In investigating the science of mind and spirit, I propose to pursue this mathematical course; and not attempt to argue any point that is not capable of demonstration—that is not based upon the absolute affirmation of the soul, conducted with reference to strict definitions, and making the relation of premises and conclusion inevitable. The reason of being thus particular is, that the greatest confusion prevails, not only in respect to the subject of the New Philosophy, or Spiritualism, but in respect to all subjects pertaining to spiritual life. Man does not know precisely where to begin his investigation. He does not seem to know precisely where he is certain of any thing pertaining to spiritual existence, and thinks that it must be all conjectural.

Now here is an affirmation which I believe every man in the audience will agree to be an affirmation of every one's consciousness, and that it lies at the basis of all our investigation of this and every other subject. (I will say further, that, if any individual in the audience disagrees with me, he will confer a favor by manifesting that disagreement at any time; because I wish to be exceedingly near to you as a lecturer, and wish you to be exceedingly near to me, so that there may be the most perfect freedom of intercourse of thought and expression between us.)

Then the first affirmation of the consciousness is this: That the mind can perceive nothing but its own consciousness, and that which is inwrought into that consciousness.

Now I wish you to try that in every possible way, to see if be true. We talk about getting information and forming ideas from subjects outside of ourselves, as though it were independent of our minds. My proposition is, that the mind can perceive nothing but its own consciousness, and that which is inwrought into that consciousness; and, furthermore, that its perception of being and existence will be according as it is inwrought into its consciousness; and by no possibility can it be anything else to the individual; and, as a matter of course, if there be any standard anywhere by which to try truth, and know that it is true, that standard must be inwrought into the consciousness of the individual who has to apply it; and he will apply it accordingly as it is inwrought into his consciousness. Now is there any one that does not perceive that this is absolutely true? Then receiving that as a truth which every mind affirms—it can not suppose the contrary of it to be true—we must set down every thing as false which conflicts with this proposition, no matter whether it overthrows authority or not. Whatever conflicts with this self-evident truth, or affirmation of universal consciousness, must be false. Truth does not conflict with truth. You may be assured that falsehood always exists where you find conflict and antagonism. It follows then, that all there is of being or of existence in the universe that will ever be known to you or me will be that which is inwrought into our consciousness. It follows, as a matter of course, the universe can be no larger and no more perfect, than it can be inwrought into our consciousness; and it will be limited to us by our mental unfolding. Hence it will necessarily follow, that different individuals who are differently unfolded in the different departments of their intellectual and perceptional natures, will perceive being and existence in very different lights; and yet each will suppose that each sees it in the same lights, until we begin to compare notes. There will be as many different New Yorks as there are different minds to form images or conceptions of New York. So there will be as many different mental Earths or mental universes as there are minds to form conceptions of our Earth and the universe; and each mind will have the Earth or the universe fashioned into his own consciousness, and when it will investigate, it will investigate that which is then fashioned therein, and study it as fashioned there. It follows then, as a matter of course, that when the image of the existence within our consciousness corresponds to the actuality, that is, when the ideal in man corresponds to the real in God, then man has the truth—not till then. That is, when my perception of being and existence corresponds with the being and existence, then I have the truth of being and existence. But just so far as my idea or perception of being or existence deviates from its actuality, just so far my impression is false. These conclusions follow as a matter of necessity. Hence you and I will learn at once, that the first lesson for us to learn in commencing the study of the universe, is to learn ourselves. The very first volume that is opened before us, is that which God has given us in giving us a conscious being. Here we must commence our first lesson, because every thing must be recorded in the pages of this volume. God can never manifest any part of the universe or himself to us beyond the capacity of the pages of this volume to receive that manifestation. It follows then, as a matter of course, that truth can never be communicated by authority; and when a man tells me that a certain thing is true upon his authority, I can not receive it simply upon his statement. You will understand that I distinguish between stating a truth and narrating a fact. I may receive a statement of fact upon authority.

A man may tell me that there is such a place as London, and I believe it; and I may form an idea respecting it; but the ideal London I have in my mind is very far from being the real London—is very far from being a representation of the real London. That is, the ideal London which I have exists only in my mind, has no representative corresponding in the outward matter-of-fact London. But when the real London is brought into my consciousness, I have *the* London. Before, I had a sort of *a* London. Now you will understand what is meant by a difference between forming a conception of a fact and a truth. Suppose I should say to you that the sum of the squares of the two sides of a right-angled triangle is equal to the square of its hypotenuse, you having faith in my capacity to determine truth will say, "I will believe it as a fact; but I have no perception of its truth—I have only your word for it." Now your faith is not in the truth of the proposition, but in my word. There is a truth there, but you can not receive it upon my authority. The reception of it as a truth depends upon your mind being unfolded to the plane of that truth. The question then for us to settle is, whether the conception in our minds corresponds to the actuality. If we have the means of determining that it does correspond, then we have the means of determining that our perception is true. The truth is the perception by the mind of that which is. You may apply this rule to any sphere of investigation that you please. Then let us begin with man as a microcosm of the universe, and who is destined in his spiritual unfolding to be a microcosm of all that is in the universe; in other words, whose mind here is to begin to translate the universe into its consciousness. The universe is a great book, which it is man's business to read and translate into his consciousness, so that the image within shall correspond to the actuality without—so that he shall be a universe of himself—so that the individual in his affection by that which is transferred also becomes a divine, a god. "Is it not written in your law, I said ye are gods?" Man is to become in his impulses and character like the divine of the universe, so that he has not only all the wisdom, fact, and principle, but all the affection of the universe, to wit, the divine translated into his affection, so that in his outward form and inward being he is a child of God, created in his image. Thus, so far as we proceed day by day in translating the actual and real universe into the perceptive and ideal in us, so fast are we unfolding and growing up into knowledge; and when that knowledge is united with the truth and affectional impulses converted into wisdom, we are made temples for the in-dwelling of the divine spirit. It becomes us, then, to make use of all means within our power to perceive this great volume that God has opened before us, and given us the means of studying, translating into our minds, and making our own. Looking at man, then, as a conscious being, one that possesses the faculty of perceiving existence in all its various modes of manifestation, and also of perceiving being itself, thus having within himself that whereon God can write not only the phenomena, but the law and science of being itself, let us become free men, lovers of the truth, determined to be honest with ourselves and the world, determined to know what can be known, and not to be deceived either by our own appetites, passions, or lusts, or by the influences that others may extend over us to turn away our minds from earnestly and truthfully investigating all subjects. The mind that is afraid to look upon the wide universe, to receive the image that God would impress upon it every day and moment of his life, is denying the birthright of his soul.

Man, as a conscious being, is the subject of three degrees of conscious perception—he can be subject to no less and no more; and being influenced by what he perceives—three degrees of affection. In other words, there is laid the foundation for three spheres of thought and three spheres of affection. He can possess no more—no less. Now I am to demonstrate this to be true in such a way that every one of you shall know its truth. I begin first to prove that these spheres of knowledge and affection exist in you, because it is my business, after having proved this—if I should succeed in proving it—to show that in the wide universe there are but those same three spheres of knowledge and those same three spheres of affection and love—no less and no more; that man possesses within himself the elements of all knowledge and affection that exist in the wide universe. Unless he did possess these elements, he could not investigate the universe; for he can only investigate that, the elements of which exist within his consciousness. In the first place, man has that faculty by which he perceives the mere phenomena of existence, or, in other words, he has that department of conscious being which is addressed by what we call the physical senses, the scope of which is to reveal to him facts and phenomena in the material plane of existence. The physical senses can only reveal to him the facts and phenomena. In this respect man differs not at all from the animal, which possesses the same number of physical senses, and is impressed by the same light that impresses man's senses—is subject to the same conditions. The law by which perception is awakened in the consciousness is the same in the animal as in the man. But man possesses also another element that is not content with mere investigation, or mere observation of forms and phenomena. You see this other nature is manifested in the little child, after he begins to walk about and observe the forms of things. There are certain things he can not ascertain by the use of the physical senses, and he asks his parents for further information. If you will examine the philosophy of asking questions, you will perceive that it is a means of gaining information by the exercise of some faculties higher than the physical senses. It is seeking for information that shall be applied to the consciousness, that shall be represented by ideas that exist in the mind. We may suppose that Sir Isaac Newton and his dog were sitting in the orchard, and that both saw an apple fall to the ground. The dog could observe the fact as well as Sir Isaac Newton, but Sir Isaac Newton perceived that there was something involved in the fall of that apple, which the dog never thought of. The dog confined his observation to the mere fact; but Sir Isaac Newton perceived, by the aid of a higher faculty, that there existed a law which he wished to ascertain, and therefore commenced investigation to discover it. This department of mind which led Sir Isaac Newton to make this investigation was not content with observing the mere facts or phenomena of existence, but wished to investigate that which was concerned in the production of the phenomenon. That faculty gives rise in man to this second sphere, which observes not the phenomena, but investigates the law or proximate causes of phenomena, and opens the field of science and philosophy. Hence the second sphere of thought is that sphere which investigates the relation of things and determines the law of action and manifestation through that relation. It belongs to what we call the relational, the middle, or mediatorial sphere; because it embraces the means by which causes operate to produce effects. For instance, I speak and you hear. I am a cause of producing a sound; your ears are affected by the sound produced. The atmosphere is the medium by which the action is transmitted from my organs of speech to those of hearing. The physical senses notice the fact in the physical sphere; the intellectual perceptions notice the means by which the fact is produced. The next, the highest, the inmost, absolute nature is that which perceives the absolute cause of these effects.

There is a sphere of mind in you that observes the mere effect; there is a sphere that investigates the relation or law by which phenomena are produced; there is also a sphere of mind which searches after and perceives the absolute cause of the phenomena. Now, inasmuch as all being or existence must come under one of these forms, either its phenomena, the means by which they are produced, or the cause which, through the means, has produced the phenomena, there can be but these three departments of conscious perception: the physical or intellectual, the moral or relational, and the divine or absolute, which perceives the absolute of all being. To illustrate the difference between the relational and the absolute: When Sir Isaac Newton discovered the existence of the law of gravitation, and found it the same that caused the motion of the planetary bodies, it was supposed that he discovered the cause of their motion. He named that law attraction, or attraction of gravitation. Now we turn upon Sir Isaac Newton and ask, What is attraction of gravitation? The only reply that can be made is to speak of its effects. However intellectual the mind may be, it must be ignorant of the absolute, because it belongs to the sphere of relations. You can not analyze the infinite. You can not compare the infinite. It is only in the sphere of the finite that the intellectual faculties have power to pursue their investigations. That which perceives the absolute must of itself be absolute; that is, the finite can not receive the infinite—the finite can not embrace the infinite. Therefore, if the infinite is ever to be represented to man, there must be a department that is receptive of the infinite; and that department must be infinite, or it can not receive the infinite. When I dwell more particularly upon this subject, I will endeavor to make it apparent to you so far as language is capable of making it.

Corresponding to the three spheres of perception there are three spheres of affection. The first sphere is called the sphere of self-love, or, to use a word which would express it in every relation, I would call it lust; that is, the desire for self-gratification. This is the lowest sphere pertaining to the finite, and corresponding to the sphere of fact or phenomena. The second sphere is the sphere of relational love, and that divides naturally into two departments—the love of unconscious nature, the love of sciences, etc., and the love of conscious being, or moral love, by which man loves his neighbor, some conscious being out of himself. That is the second sphere of love, known as relational, and it belongs to the sphere of relational truth, or the sphere of intellectual and moral investigation. There is a third sphere of impulse or love, known as the divine or absolute love, called the love of God, the love of the infinite. In one of these three spheres is every man's ruling affection to be found—in the sphere of self-love, seeking self-gratification; or in the sphere of moral love, seeking the welfare of his neighbor; or in the sphere of divine love, loving as God loves, universally—not objectively, but subjectively, all the wide universe. There can be but just these three spheres. Now if each of you will investigate, you will readily recognize two of the affections at least to which I have called your attention, self-love, and social love, but more particularly self-love, desire for self-gratification, desiring that you may be first mad happy, and then leaving the world to be happy afterward. The love that goes out of itself, and loves some being out of yourself, is exemplified in the love of a true husband for his wife, of a parent for his child, of a brother for a sister. All these loves give indication of the second sphere of love, known as charity, good-will to the neighbor. This love is the means by which self-love is first overcome or destroyed. The individual is brought from self-love, through charity, to divine love, just as, in his knowledge, he is brought from the sphere of fact, through relation, to the absolute of being; and hence, in the spheres of unfolding, the three degrees are necessarily absolute. Look at society. What is it but the aggregate of individuals composing it? Society, separate from individuals, is nothing. The love of society is only the love of the aggregate of individuals. Now, inasmuch as the love will belong either to the sphere of self-love, charity, or divine love, you will find that society will always be expressive of one of these three loves, never the third, though. We say of society, when we look to the principles that govern it in its administration, it is but the embodiment of the character and will of those constituting the government —it is but an expression of the individuals composing it. Therefore there are three spheres of government corresponding to the three spheres of the individual. For individuals living in the selfish nature, the government will be a government of force. The individual who has come out of this obeys the truth because he loves the truth. He does not feel the restraints of law that says, Thou shalt not steal, Thou shalt not lie. He does not know that there are any such laws in the

State. He never felt any restraints. That individual is not in the sphere of self-love; and the government over him is not a government of force. The government over him is a moral government, and has its place in his affection.

Coming out of the government of force, man comes into the second, the Christian, or government of moral love, the government of charity. He then comes under the "new commandment I give unto you, that ye love one another." This second, or mediatorial sphere, is a moral one; hence this dispensation has been called the mediatorial dispensation. Hence I say there will be a second sphere of government, or second dispensation, as it was called; but that dispensation is only the magnification of the individual. It is only the representation of society as one great individual. Then there is a prophecy of the third and perfect dispensation, which is called the millennial, the divine dispensation. When the second shall have performed its mediatorial work, when every individual will have been perfected in his moral nature, and shall be prepared to receive influx from the divine, then will arise the third dispensation of government, known as the millennial. If we refer to the forms of expression by which it is designated, we will find it spoken of as taking place at the consummation of the age, at the end of the world, when that mediatorial age is through, when man is perfected in his moral nature, has put down all rule and power; then Christ himself becomes subject to the Father, and God, the Divine, becomes all in all. That brings in the third dispensation, the third sphere of government. These three spheres of love in man lay the foundation for the spheres exhibited in the Spirit-world. The governments upon the earth, as well as in heaven, have their basis in man. Man is but the footings-up of all past ages; and the Spiritual worlds have their foundation in him. Therefore, when you and I wish to study the Spirit-spheres, to know what constitutes a sphere and degree, we are not obliged to go out of ourselves and look into space ten, fifteen, or a thousand miles away. That is not the way to study the Spirit-world. The way is to go within and study the spheres of Spiritual being and affection. Individuals who are in either of these spheres are allied to one of the three spheres in the Spiritual world. The first is called the lowest, or dark sphere, the sphere of outer darkness, sometimes called the grave. The grave was called the place of darkness, where there was neither knowledge, or device, or wisdom, and was that to which allusion was made in saying, that those in the graves shall hear the voice of God, and shall live. It is sometimes called "Gehenna." It corresponds to man's lustful nature, and represents the darkness and impurity of man under the influence of his lusts. That is what characterizes the first or lowest sphere of Spiritual being. The second sphere corresponds to man's intellectual or moral nature. It is called "Paradise," the place of happiness. Jesus said to the thief on the cross, "To-day shalt thou be with me in Paradise." Two days after, when Mary met him at the tomb, and offered to embrace him, he said, "Touch me not, for I have not yet ascended to my Father."

He had been in Paradise—in the second sphere—and he told them that when he ascended to his Father they should see him no more. Both Gehenna and Paradise are spheres of Spirit-manifestation. Those who are charitable, and who do possess truly spiritual natures or affections, are in alliance with Paradise. Those in lust are in alliance with the sphere of lust or Gehenna. Those who have passed through, and fulfilled every impulse and every love in the second sphere, are said then to be brought into the divine presence. They no longer need a middle man between them and the Divine, because the Father can then speak directly to them. But so long as man is in the sphere of outer darkness or in Paradise, there is between him and the Divine (and he must approach by a mediator) something that can take the things of the Father and make them manifest to him in the visible sense. But when man has come into the third sphere, there is no longer a middle man; Christ himself becomes subject to the Father, and God becomes all in all. Then comes the New Dispensation, or the Consummation of the Christian Age. The point to which I wish to call your attention is, that the governments in earth, as well as in heaven, all have their basis in man — man being but the footings-up of all the ages of eternity. All is summed up in him; and he is the footings-up of all that preceded him; hence all the Spiritual spheres have their basis in man. Therefore, when we wish to study the Spirit-spheres, we are not obliged to go out of ourselves and begin to look off into space ten, fifteen, or one thousand miles away. The way is to come within, and ascertain the sphere of Spiritual being, Spiritual perception and affection; for all there is of the Spiritual universe is what has its basis in the individual Spirits who constitute the spheres.

As the societies of earth are composed of the individuals of earth, so are the spheres of the heavens composed of the individuals of the heavens, and the ruling nature of the different spheres is but the aggregate of the ruling loves of those composing those spheres. The laws of the spheres are but the laws of those composing the spheres. We are germinal universes. We are to be developed and unfolded consciously till the whole universe is translated into our consciousness. There is but one way to study the universe, and that is to come down into ourselves and study ourselves. This idea of looking out of ourselves, looking to any external method outside of our consciousness to find out what constitutes a Spiritual sphere or degree, is all fallacious. Spirits may come and rap, talk, and preach till doomsday; if they can not find the elements within your consciousness out of which they can construct that Spiritual sphere, you can not perceive or get any true idea of Spirit-spheres. It is as though I were born blind, and had never seen the light, and of course knew nothing of light, color, and darkness, and some individual should endeavor to make me believe that I was living in total darkness, when there would be no part of my being to which he could appeal to make me believe. There would be no possibility of conveying the thought to my mind, because I should have no conscious experience of light, color, etc. Outward language could not give me the idea. Unless I have had the conscious experience to give me the idea out of which to construct the idea, the Spirits from the Spirit-world may come from every sphere and degree, and they can not convey to my mind an accurate idea of those spheres and degrees. If they would make me understand who God is, and what he is, they must find in me the elements out of which to construct that God. I say it is useless to look for information out of yourselves until you know what is in yourselves. The first lesson is to learn who and what am I. I propose to commence my investigations in each individual's own consciousness, starting with affirmations of that consciousness, and with definitions about which we can not disagree, and then go forward step by step, demonstrating every point, and ascertaining the law of manifestation as that law is revealed in us. I do not ask Spirits, and do not wish them to come to tell me about the law that governs in their sphere. The truth is, we can not avoid the fact, that all communications that come understandingly, must come in the method that God has ordained, and that method is that it must be written by his law upon our consciousness; and when it is written so, Spirits can come and point out the writing to us; and that is the best they can do. I desire you to understand distinctly what will be the basis of my lectures, what will be the points I shall attempt to establish. I shall endeavor to prove Spiritualism. I shall not come to the raps for a considerable time. They are so far off, I shall not attempt to prove Spiritualism by rapping for some time yet. People say we have got beyond the rapping. The truth is, a large portion of the world have not yet got to the raps. They are not yet able to appreciate the raps. We must make considerable progress before we can get the philosophy of the raps. We have much to learn yet before we can get the full benefit of a simple sound, even though it be not accompanied by much intelligence. The first lesson I shall attempt to teach—pardon me for assuming to be a teacher, I will be a pupil at any time—is how to study and know yourselves; how to ascertain the laws of your being, action, and manifestation; how to determine what is and what is not spiritual in you; how to determine whether you are under Spirit-influence or not—for there are laws by which all these things can be determined. In my investigation I shall perhaps be able to determine where that terrible creature, Jack, the Giant-killer, the Odylic force, resides, and show what it can and what it can not do. And I promise, too, in the face and eyes of all theorizers who believe that the Spiritual manifestations are traceable to this force, and to the satisfaction of everybody else, to demonstrate that it is not competent to produce them. I will demonstrate it according to President Mahan's hypothesis. I will show by every known law of nature that the power exerted at the brain's center, in a single instance he has given, was equal to a thousand steam-engines of a million horse-power at the distance of five feet from the brain. But that will merely come in as collateral when I consider the objections offered to our theory. I will endeavor to consider every objection which any objector has proposed to bring forward. I do not stand here to boast, but what I speak is to me absolute. I stand here fearlessly, and invite all classes of minds to raise any objection they can to the Spiritual theory; and I bind myself to answer them instanter, or confess my inability to do so. The invitation commences now, and extends to every moment I am in the city.

In my next lecture I shall begin with the question of Spirit-spheres, and endeavor to unfold to the consciousness of each of you the evidence of the existence of a first sphere, from which you will all do well to escape; and shall then proceed to prove the existence of other spheres, namely, the second, or relational sphere, and a third, or divine sphere. I invite skeptics and atheists in particular to be particularly captious.

CHAPTER II.
THE SPHERE OF LUST.

Man possesses three natures—the animal or sensuous nature, the intellectual and moral nature, and the divine nature. Mind, in whatever department it is manifested, possesses two qualities—perception and affection, and understanding and love; or, when understanding is united with true affection, wisdom and love. I have heretofore said, that since man, in the lowest department of his being, is animal in his character, possessing the faculty of perceiving facts and phenomena, that faculty was the perceptive part of his animal being which embraces self-love, or a desire after self-gratification. That portion of the mind which pertains to the second part of man's nature was described as being that which investigates the laws and relation of things, inquires into what relates to that department of nature called the scientific, and studies that which relates to man and society. What is called the moral department of man's being is that which relates to the affectional part of his nature, and which is called moral love or charity. That which pertains to the divine or absolute of man's being was said to embrace the religious element in him; through which department the Infinite, as the absolute of being and of affection, is to be revealed to the mind. The love characterizing this department was described as divine love —the love of the Divine Being. The first love is objective in self, the second is objective in neighbor, and the third is subjective in God. Thus, then, was given the division of that department of mind pertaining to man's perception and affection.

I am now to commence with the first—man in the lowest department of his perception and affection, to show you its nature, and its presence in him, in society, in government, and in the Spirit-world. If we would learn the laws that govern in that sphere of the Spirit-world called outer darkness, we need only learn the laws that govern in the sphere of outer darkness which is in man, and which is caused by man to exist in society. A singular idea has obtained, that this lower animal nature derives its quality from the physical body we carry about with us; and that when we come to be separated from it, we shall no longer possess any of that nature; as though this earthly body was the foundation of perception or affection—as though the instrument were the cause—as though this body, which we temporarily inhabit, exercised more control over us than the mind!

I propose first, then, to inquire how much influence the body exercises upon the mind, and how much influence the mind exercises upon the body, so that we may arrive at something like an accurate conclusion as to what our condition will be beyond the grave; for if we know how much is to be subtracted, at death, from our animal natures, we can know how much of that nature remains after we have passed beyond the influence of these material bodies. My first position is this: The manifestation of impulse in finite beings rises out of the relation which one finite being sustains to another. There is no impulse that does not grow out of this relation; and the impulse is according to the nature and character of that relation. In the divine order, if my body, as a physical and a finite existence, did not sustain any relation, it would be subject to no impulse; therefore, whenever I perceive an impulse arising within me, I am informed thereby that I sustain a certain relation to something, and that if I would become truly wise in controlling that impulse, I must learn what that relation is. I might begin back of mind or conscious being to show how uniform this law is in the material or unconscious world, as that the influence between the earth and the sun arises out of a certain relation existing between them, and that if you change or destroy that relation, you change or destroy that influence. But I will illustrate this truth by reference to a conscious being. If man could be isolated from all laws, he would be a very different being from what he now is, although he might retain the same constitution which he now possesses; because he could not then come into certain relations which are necessary, in order to have revealed within him certain affections. I will take, for instance, the conjugal relation. It is the nearest the Divine. It is the first-begotten relation below the Infinite. Until a man and woman come into the true conjugal relation, they can not experience that love known as conjugal love. Till then it can not be begotten in them. They may conjecture they know what it is, but until that true relation is established between them, they can never have an adequate conception of it—can never know what it is to become so oblivious in another as the true wife does in the husband, or the true husband does in the wife; nor can they, like the true husband and wife, experience that perfect harmony of soul, or listen to that sweet spiritual music within, till they have entered this relation, which alone can fit them for a proper conjugal union. The law exists, and the conditions exist; but man must place himself, and woman must place herself, within the sphere of the law and the conditions, or they can not experience the benefit to be derived from them. So with the parental relation. No woman can know what maternal love is till she becomes a mother. Is it not so, mothers? People may conjecture that they know what it is, and suppose it to be a pure and friendly love-feeling existing between mother and child; but they can have no adequate conception of the deep tenderness and holiness of maternal love—their idea of it does not begin to reach down into the almost infinite depths of that holy love. There is no possible way for an individual to know what maternal love is, but to come into the maternal relation. That is the way God reveals it in the soul. The reason is, that the true maternal impulse in the finite is the manifestation of the Divine in the finite sphere, and this manifestation can only be made in an individual when that individual comes into the sphere where the Infinite can confer that blessing. The same is true with reference to paternal, fraternal, filial, and social love: they all depend for their development upon those in whom they are manifested coming into the true relation which gives birth to them.

The same law holds good when applied to the relations existing between the body and the spirit. My body can not be nourished so as to become an instrument of individualizing in me an immortal spirit, unless it be sustained by those things necessary to become a part of its organism. I have needs, as an immortal being, which must be supplied, or I perish; and since those needs exist, they must have some means of manifesting themselves to me; and one of the means employed for that purpose is the feeling of hunger. A desire for food proclaims a need of my wasting body. The needed material can then be taken into it to build it up and fit it for its holy mission of being an instrument in elaborating an immortal spirit. So, likewise, thirst is the voice of God proclaiming a need of my body, and my spirit is induced to seek for that which shall supply the demand of a divine impulse originating in that plane. So it is in regard to all other needs of the body calling upon the spirit for gratification. The impulses, then, pertaining to this body have not their origin in this body, but only in the relation which this body sustains to my spirit; and when the spirit has fulfilled its duty of supplying the needs of the body, the demand ceases. When, being hungry, I have appropriated the proper quantity of food, the desire for food ceases. It is so respecting every other need—when it is supplied, the demand ceases, and the individual continues to be satisfied till the demand is again created. By studying the needs of the body, and making yourself acquainted with its condition as far as it relates to the spirit, you may learn exactly how much influence, truly and properly, it exerts upon your spirit; but when you look beyond the needs of the body, and find impulses asking for more, you may be certain that you are finding impulses which do not pertain to your body. Though they may lay hold of your body and stimulate it to action and administer to its gratification, yet they do not arise out of it, but out of some neglected need. Such impulses are the voice of God calling our attention to some need which you have forgotten or neglected, and they will not permit you to rest till you discover what that need is and supply it. I will illustrate this point.

Although man in the lower department of his nature is animal, he is nevertheless something more than an animal in the activities of his nature. The highest impulse of the animal is to provide for and protect its perishable mortal structure, and he has no immortal spirit to provide for in the future. He is content when the needs of the body are supplied. Did you never notice how content and unconcerned are the horse and dog when their demand for food is supplied? Young animals and young children, in their play, are supplying one of the needs of their body. But when the children have passed from childhood, desires of that kind cease, if they become properly developed men and women, and others take their place; while the animal, whenever the needs of his animal nature are supplied, is satisfied. Consequently, you do not see dissipated animals. Did you ever think of that? Animals do not get drunk, nor seek for gratification in any such unnatural channel. Animals are true to nature and to God. They can not have thoughts and desires that pertain to the undying spirit, their highest nature being merely animal. Were man as true to all the needs of his being as is the animal to the needs of his animal nature, he would not be the discontented, unhappy, and lustful being he now is. But in consequence of having to supply the needs of a higher nature, he finds himself far from being as contented as the brute, whose animal wants are all provided for.

There are spiritual needs pertaining to his understanding and affections which are entirely overlooked or neglected by him, whose demands are as imperative as are the demands of the animal nature. The demands of his intellectual and moral nature cause him to feel the lack of something within which destroys his rest and quiet. He seeks to satisfy this lack by gratifying his sensuous appetites and passions. Thus man runs into vice, and becomes sinful. Were it not for his immortal thirsting for the water of life, he never would be a wicked, lustful being; or if he would *supply* the demands of that thirst, he never would be discontented or lustful.

Now let us make the distinction between the lustful and the divine impulse, that you may better understand what I mean by the sphere to which I am calling your attention. We all can tell the difference by appealing to our own consciousness. The divine impulse informs us of a need, and leads us to seek to supply it. The Infinite only speaks of needs, and leads man to supply them, that he may grow up into a perfect being. Every impulse in man, from the lowest to the highest nature, must be attended to, in order to render him perfect. The true impulse is one that promotes individual happiness and contentment.

When the infant, in consequence of this impulse, feels the sense of hunger calling for food, and such food as its infantile nature requires, it cries; but the supply of that demand is only necessary to cause it to cease its crying. This is because the child is free from those lusts which attach to persons advanced in years. "Of such is the kingdom of heaven." The child does not lust after things that shall gratify or tickle its palate; it only seeks for those things which it needs; and when they are supplied, it ceases calling for more. But with the advance of age it learns of lustful parents, or by being acted upon by lustful influences, to seek gratification through lust, while in its original unperverted state it knows no impulses but those which are natural, and, consequently, it obeys the true and divine law.

Without stopping to inquire into the origin of lust, I may say that it originates in man's ignorance, necessarily. If you recollect the figure in the parable of the Garden of Eden, you remember that the sin committed by Eve was eating of the tree of knowledge of good and evil. That is where we all eat. But I do not propose to dwell upon the nature and origin of this lust in man, but merely to speak of it as being that which characterizes him in his lowest sphere of being. It brings him into antagonism with his neighbor and God. It is that which begets in him so much crime, and which brings ruin upon the world. That is lust which leads him to seek after self-gratification irrespective of any need, while the true impulse only leads him to seek to supply those things which are *really* needed. The impulse belonging to the lower sphere may be characterized as lust. The idea which obtains so generally in society, that lust belongs only to animal, sensual, or sexual desires, is, therefore, erroneous.

Man may seek gratification in every plane of his being; not only in what he eats and drinks, but also in the intellectual plane. He may seek to gratify a vain curiosity. When he feels restless, he goes off searching after amusement. Time hangs heavy on his soul. There is a perishing need calling for action, and he knows not whence it comes, and he seeks to "kill" this time by amusement or otherwise. This is lusting, not in the animal sense, but in the intellectual sense. He may also lust in the moral plane. What are called friendships in the world, are distinguished by lusts. You know how the world selects its friends: it selects them according to the pleasure it expects to derive from them. Is it not so? Does not the selfish man and woman select friends with reference to the enjoyment they expect to derive from their association with them? And are they not most constant in their attention to those who are most successful in administering to their enjoyment? Look at this, each of you. Look over the list of your friends, and tell me *really* what is the basis of your friendship. You love your friends, you say. Why do you love them? You love to be with them. Why? You seek their society. Why? Some of your friends you love best. Tell me why it is that you love them best. You say they are the most agreeable to you, and hence you love to be with them. Is that the highest basis? If so, when they cease to administer to your gratification, what relation will you hold to them then? It is said that "prosperity makes friends, and adversity tries them." They can make it pleasant for us when they are with us, and in prosperity; but when adversity comes, their position is not quite high enough for us; and we prefer those differently conditioned. This remark is in accordance with the statement, that the friendship of the world is based upon the principle of gratifying ourselves. In making your morning calls, you sometimes visit your friends from a sense of duty; and are influenced by the fear that they will find fault with you if you follow your feelings in the matter, and go where you will derive the greatest amount of pleasure.

When you think these friends are laboring to your disadvantage, then your love for them soon cools off. They don't answer your purpose. Thus, trifling circumstances make foes of friends. You may test the friendship you think you have for individuals. If a person's friendship seems to be strong, and he can not enjoy his friendship for another, unless in that other's society, and he desires to be in the presence of that person, so that he can hear his voice and feel his personal influence, and if, when separated from that friend he is disquieted and unhappy, very much as is the person who uses strong drink or tobacco, and is deprived of his beer, or rum, or tobacco —his friendship has a low basis. But if one has a true friendship, which is high, and holy, and spiritual, one where his whole confidence is merged in that friend, he trusts him with his heart and most secret thoughts, and knows without doubt that he can not be betrayed by that friend; and they hold constant spiritual communion with each other, no matter how far apart— there is a concord of spiritual communion between them that enables them to enjoy each other's society when separated by hundreds of miles. True friendship is of the spiritual kind that does not regard so gross and physical a friendship as the friendship of the world. I wish to call your attention to the presence of this impulse in you, because perhaps you have not looked at the subject in this light.

A word to husbands and wives. A young man, when he contemplates getting married, thinks he will get a wife that will make him very happy. One young man thinks he would like a wife who will be economical; another, one who would make a good housekeeper; and another, an intellectual companion; so they select not so much with reference to the wife, as to the use of the wife. And ladies, on the other hand, select husbands who they think will provide them a good home, afford them protection, etc.; they want a husband for his use; so the union between the man and woman is often based upon the idea of use, and not upon their fitness for companions; and hence their love for each other continues so long as the use continues, and no longer. If a man who desires a good housekeeper finds that his wife is not one, or if a husband finds his wife faulty in any other important particular, just in proportion as she proves faulty his love for her is abated; and at the end of twenty-eight days—the period denominated the *"honey-moon"*—he finds he does not love her near as well as he supposed; and that what he supposed was love, was, after all, but a desire after gratification—that he was loving self instead of his wife.

Man may be lustful in his religion as well as in his moral relations. He may mistake what he supposes to be the love of God for the love of the use of God. He expects God is going to make him eternally happy, and bestow upon him unending enjoyment, and for this reason he shouts and praises him, and calls it loving God. He does not see that God is so much better than anybody else; but he has become satisfied that God means well, and will bless him; and he honors him for these things. Hence his seeking after religion that he may make himself happy and save himself from suffering is as lustful and selfish as seeking after something good to eat or drink, making self-gratification the object of his search. The great difficulty, my friends, with popular religion is, that it is only a religious expression of lust. That it has not beaten swords into plowshares and spears into pruning-hooks, and taught people to learn war no more, is because it has failed to adopt the means by which the world can be made pure and happy. Hence the religious man may be as selfish as the miserly man, and yet think he is so much like God that he is going to be saved. But it is not religion that he loves; it is only the use of religion. Satisfy him that God is not going to benefit him, but that he is going to damn him, and he will curse him bravely. I ask everybody to look at this.

It is claimed, as I have already remarked, that the impulse of lust belongs to the body, and does not grow out of the relation which the mind sustains to the body. What need, I ask, did Alexander's body feel, which demanded that he should have all the kings and potentates of earth on their knees before him? What did he want of the wealth of the earth? and what made him weep because there was not another world to conquer? Was it his body? I tell you, Nay; there were perishing needs within him that would not give him rest till they were supplied; and, ignorant of the nature of those needs, he sought to supply them by the gratification of his selfish nature. Not heeding the voice of God, he took his sword and rushed upon mankind, and made that the balm for the healing of his restless spirit; and when he had conquered the world, and had it at his command, he was more miserable than before; simply because he had entered farther into the broad road leading to destruction and death. He felt the bitter agony of soul consequent upon a departure from the straight and narrow path. This lust was not the lust of his body—it was the lust of the spirit. It was a desire for self-gratification that arose, because the needs existing in consequence of neglecting the demands of the spirit were not supplied. He sought gratification in a way in which he thought he could obtain it; but he was sadly disappointed in the result.

The miser, in every age, has been trying to obtain happiness by getting gold. A French miser, who, like a great mass of mankind, thought wealth would make him happy, sought for it, and was so successful as to obtain it. He possessed his untold millions, and yet desired more; and he found that the more he possessed the more he desired. He also perceived that his wealth did not gratify his wants. The moment he possessed it, he found he could not take care of it to his liking. He could not trust it in banks, for the banks might break; and he did not like to invest it in stocks, for stocks were liable to depreciate in value; so he made up his mind that he would convert it into money, and keep it continually in his sight; and accordingly he had it placed in heaps, and stood and watched it. But then he was unable to sleep because he feared burglars and assassins, whose plottings for his life and money constantly rung in his ear. As he stood and watched those shining heaps, he reflected that although he had obtained wealth he had derived no satisfaction from it, but that every dollar added to his possessions added a new pang to his sorrows; and he determined to kill himself, and accordingly proceeded to the banks of the river Seine, for the purpose of drowning himself. Upon arriving at the river's bank, happening to put his hand in his pocket, he found four guineas. Thinking they would thereafter be of no use to him, he concluded that rather than have them lost, he would, before he sought his watery grave, go and find some needy person to whom he might give the money. He accordingly went to a miserable hovel close by. As he approached it, he heard cries of agony and distress within. He entered, when he beheld a most heart-rending sight. There lay a poor, sick, distressed widow on a pallet of straw, with a few rags for covering; and there were four hungry, dirty, naked children crying for bread, while the sick mother had no bread for them, or the means of obtaining any. The miser stepped up to the bed, and placed the four strayed guineas in her hand, and told her they were hers. She looked wildly at the money, and then at the giver, and then at the guineas again. She seized his hand, pressed it, blessed him, and called upon God to bless him; and the children thanked him. The thanks, and blessings, and tears which were showered upon that miser's heart caused it to break, and for the first time in his life a pulsation of pleasure, delight, and satisfaction beat through his soul, and as he stood and witnessed the joy, and thankfulness, and hope of that family he exclaimed, "What! is happiness so cheap? then I will be happy." Then he went away, not to drown himself in the Seine, but to seek out other similar cases of suffering; and after that he had no occasion to kill himself, for he had found what was the canker that had so long been gnawing upon his heart. He found that he possessed a moral nature that had needs, and that that nature was calling upon him to perform certain moral duties; and that the moment he obeyed the demands of that nature, he silenced that clamoring within, which had all his life long rendered him unhappy and discontented; and at a good old age he testified that the way to be happy was to be good and useful.

I think his experience will be yours and mine. We talk about wanting pleasure, and we seek it in amusements and at theaters, routs, and balls; and I tell you that this feeling arises from the same cause as the miser's misery. We have hungerings and thirstings of soul which we are required to satisfy, and except we comply with these requirements we will be disquieted. If those of you who love the opera, the theater, etc., will go forth and tread these streets, and find out the objects of need—those worthy of aid—and visit them, and administer to their comfort, you will no longer feel the need of theaters, routs, and balls; and you will find greater satisfaction in such a course than these amusements can afford. Try the experiment, and I will guarantee you will be successful. That this city, like all great cities, is pursuing after pleasure, as the paramount object to be attained, is because their souls are hungering and thirsting after that food necessary to build them up into the stature of perfect men and women. This makes time seem cruel, and hang heavy upon them; and, like the victim who seeks to drown his sorrow in the cup, they seek to fill up the long hours in dissipation. To return to my subject.

This sphere of lust, I say, then, does not arise from the body, nor from the influence of the body on the soul. It arises from our neglect of our spiritual needs. This lust, this desire proclaims a divine life within, which demands activity corresponding to our real natures; and we can never get peace and happiness until those real demands of our natures are supplied. I appeal to all pleasure-seekers whether this is not true. You have heard it argued whether there be more pleasure in anticipation than in participation. The world's pleasures are always in the future, never in the present. The man or the woman of the world is never satisfied with present conditions or present attainments. Why not? Because the man and the woman of the world are not attending to the present needs of the spiritual nature. The finite man ought to understand that he lives only in the present. God the Infinite only belongs to the future. Man's needs pertain to to-day. His physical, moral, and intellectual needs are all bearing upon the present, and not the future. The past is his schoolmaster, to teach him how to be ready to enjoy the future. It is to-day that we should take thought for; hence the divine saying of the man of Nazareth—"Take no thought for the morrow. Sufficient unto the day is the evil thereof." If we look to the present, and supply the needs of the present, the future will take care of itself. The man seeking for religion thinks he wants it for the future, in order that he may die right; but a man does not want religion to die by. There will be no trouble about his dying if he only lives right. I do not care for religion for the sake of having it to die by. Only give me its living benefits, and you are welcome to its dying benefits. This shows the false estimate the world sets upon religion.

I desire to impress upon your minds this principle, that when you look down to the real basis of selfishness and lust, you will find that they do not originate in the body, but that they pertain to the spiritual being. There are certain needs, however, which do grow out of the physical body; but when the spirit is separated from the body, it no longer feels these physical demands; for instance, it will no longer feel the need of food, experience thirst, or be susceptible to the effects of the elements—heat and cold—as is the physical nature; but that which administers to the demands of the mind, independent of the body, belongs to the mind. And when you enter the Spirit world, if you take truth with you, you will also take falsehood—if you carry purity with you, so you will impurity—if justice goes with you to that sphere, so will injustice. Now think of society in its individual action, social, governmental, and religious action, and tell me whether the world, or the individuals of the world, are governed by the true, divine impulse? Are they searching after the true needs of the body and mind, or after pleasure and self-gratification? And in your activity, which controls?—a sense of need, or a desire after gratification? You settle this question for yourselves, and I will settle it for myself. If you are under the rule, and in the sphere, of lust you belong to the sphere of outer darkness; and if you are under the rule of charity, you belong to the second sphere or Spiritual Paradise. His servants you are to whom you yield yourselves servants to obey. It is for you to say whom you will obey.

Now this earthly sphere is the lowest and darkest sphere. Its influences are dark and defiling. In this sphere men are swallowed up in worldly matters, and striving to gratify self.

But when a separation takes place between the mind and the body, we shall come into new relations, although we shall not at once change our thoughts, feelings, and affections, and shall recognize ourselves. Our lusts and self-love will follow us to the Spirit-world. There is not, as many seem to suppose, a miraculous process, by which man is changed while passing through the dark valley of shadows. If a change takes place in him in the Spirit-world, it must be in accordance with the same divine law which governs him in this sphere of existence. If you will but exercise your reasoning faculties on this point, you will see that it should and must be so. When we come to understand the Spirit-world, we shall find that in our Father's house there is a mansion suited to those who seek after self-gratification, and that that world, like this, is subdivided into many minor spheres, corresponding to the various grades of development in the different spheres of mind. There are physical spheres, intellectual spheres, moral spheres, and religious spheres, as there are in this world; and they are very much of the some description as those here, because they proceed from the same basis. Individuals passing from this sphere to that, will fashion out of the materials which their own conscious elements furnish the same kind of a Deity there that they worshiped here. As in New York city there are many degrees of advancement in these different departments—one man seeking to gratify his lusts through appetite, and another man in some other way; and as you can find here every sphere, except the divine sphere (I doubt whether you can find that), so in the Spiritual world you will find all these different degrees of advancement, each occupying its own appropriate sphere.

Here is one man who seeks gratification, it may be, in strong drink, and he worships the bowl; another seeks it in food, and hence becomes an epicure, and worships the stomach; another, it may be, seeks gratification in practicing certain games or tricks, or following after some amusement; while another seeks gratification in sexual indulgences. So you may go on and enumerate the endless variety of channels in which men seek to gratify their selfish desires; and it will be found that those in the same pursuit affinitize with one another—drunkards with drunkards, etc.—every sphere delighting in that which corresponds to the desires of those who compose it. So in the Spirit-world; the Spirit who was a drunkard here seeks gratification in the same direction that he did on earth; the seeker of pleasure there still has a love for the theater, routs, and balls; the libertine still delights in miserable songs he was accustomed to hear.

Governments, institutions, and associations and relations, whether social, spiritual, or otherwise, are expressions of what are the loves and delights of the soul of man. Therefore, in all institutions, you will find displayed the characters of those who founded them. The government of any country is but the child of the ruling mind or minds of that country. Then, if we wish to understand the dark spheres in the Spiritual world, we have only to drop the body and have our spiritual eyes opened, when we will see that there exist there all the phases of society that we find here. The cause of this arises from the sphere of lust. You have there your gambling Spirits, your drinking Spirits, your lustful Spirits, etc. And how do these poor creatures live there? That is the next question. What do they do to gratify their desires? I will tell you. You understand it to be a psychological principle, that when two men are brought into sympathy, or into *rapport* with each other (one being positive and the other negative), feelings, sensations, and desires can be communicated from one to the other. To give an illustration: You have seen, in mesmerism, an exhibition of mind separated from the influences of the body. When the mind is thus separated, and this mesmeric sympathy is established between the subject and the operator, any surgical operation can be performed upon the subject without giving him pain, because his being of sensation is removed from his body; but you can not pull the hair of the operator, or hurt his finger, or otherwise give him pain, without giving pain to the subject. Whatever the operator enjoys or suffers, the subject also enjoys and suffers. Now it is in accordance with this principle that Spirits of the other world gratify their desires. Spirits who visit this world are obliged to make use of and come into *rapport* with, those who have appetites and desires similar to their own. If the mind is separated from its own body, it can experience the sensations of another body with which it may come into *rapport*. On the same principle a good mind, or, if you please, the Divine Mind, can flow into the individual mind, and impart thought and sensation to that mind. Or a good Spirit can flow into a medium, and awaken sensations and thoughts in accordance with the law of action and re-action, becoming negative or positive, according as he wishes to impart or receive influence. Here, then, is the means by which the Spirit is enabled to gratify its desires by visiting earth. Those Spirits who allow themselves to be influenced by their lusts are called tempting Spirits, and they influence individuals on earth that they may make use of them as a means of gratifying these lusts. The same law is manifested by individuals in the body. It is not because Spirits wish to injure the bodies which they thus use, but because they desire self-gratification, and know of no other means of obtaining it, except in this sphere of outer darkness. The lowest in this scale of unfolding corresponds to this lustful nature in man. Every affection in society that can affect societies of men has its representative in the individual man; so that every subdivision of the sphere of lust has its representative in each individual; and the question is whether he lives in one of these departments or another. If I am developed in the moral department, there I live, and love, and worship; and when I pass to the Spirit-world, I go to a sphere corresponding to that ruling affection by which I am controlled. So it is in regard to any other sphere of unfolding, whether it be relational or absolute, or otherwise. Hence man himself determines his sphere. Take any man or woman you please, and let them be developed to any sphere, from the darkest sphere of lust to the purest sphere of love, and if there is any place in God's universe where they can find that which corresponds to that lust or love, they will find it. If there is any condition suited to make them happy, they will find it. If this were not so, the Spirit-world would be the worst hell imaginable. To compel a man to go where he has no affinity would be to inflict upon him one of the greatest punishments conceivable. Compel a lustful libertine to remain in a Methodist class-meeting, and shout and sing with the enthusiastic Methodists, and he would be extremely miserable—he could find many places where he would be infinitely more happy; and in order to be happy, he would be obliged to go where he could find that which would correspond to his cast of mind. We can determine where a man's God is when we ascertain what it is to which he will sacrifice every thing else.

After having thus given the law governing this lowest sphere of the Spirit-world, which represents man in his undeveloped nature as an intellectual and moral being—we are qualified to comprehend that sphere, and understand that the same spheres of mind which belong to this belong also to the Spiritual world, and that undeveloped Spirits from that lust-sphere visit earth, or societies of earth, not for the purpose of redeeming them, but for the purpose of seeking their own gratification. I have presented to you my views of that sphere as I understand it, and I shall be prepared, in my next lecture, to take up the second sphere, and tell you what constitutes it, and how it is that it becomes a mediatorial sphere—middle sphere. This second, or Spiritual sphere, is between the dark and light, or divine sphere. It is the means through which the lustful are brought out of their lusts to the divine.

CHAPTER III.
THE SECOND, OR RELATIONAL SPHERE.

The subject now to be considered is that of the second sphere of mind, both in its perceptions and affections. Our last discourse was upon what we denominated the first sphere, which was characterized as being a sphere of self-love or lusting after self-gratification. The individual in this sphere was described as being in the lowest department of his mind, and as allied in his affinities with the lowest pleasures of existence. It was remarked that this plane of lust could be manifested as well in the intellectual, moral, and religious plane, as in the animal or physical plane. The criterion by which we determine whether it is selfishness is to inquire whether the motive prompting to activity has for its object desire after gain. If this is the ruling impulse, then the individual's love is the love of self. Though the grossness of the lust may depend upon the direction given it, yet it is essentially the same whether exercised in the moral, intellectual, or physical plane. An individual who sought the happiness of another without reference to his own interests was described as belonging to the second sphere. He would seek association by the affinity of his moral or second-sphere nature.

We meet with individuals in society who affirm that man is essentially selfish—that he can not conceive a wish which does not originate in a desire for self-gain. I have no doubt that the individuals making that affirmation are very honest in it, and speak from their own conscious experience. There are many such to be found in society, who know no higher love than self-love, and their highest benevolence is based upon selfishness. I doubt not that there are those who entertain such sentiments, but I utterly protest when such men attempt to speak for the Race. I will allow every person to speak for himself upon this point, and to ascertain if there are not some actions which have not this lustful basis; and when we find that there are such actions arising within ourselves which are not contaminated with this selfish thought, and which go forth to seek expression out of ourselves, we may know that they do not belong to the first, but to the second sphere of action, I mean the sphere of relation, as separate from the individual considered in his individual love or individual selfish impulse. I will give a few illustrations of this kind.

Every individual coming under the divine impulses of the sphere of relation—I mean relation in its divine order—and living in forgetfulness of separate self, will experience some of the impulses which belong to that sphere. When the mother comes into the maternal relation and experiences the love of a mother for her child, she is ready to sacrifice the comforts and interests of self for the welfare of that object that sustains that near and dear relation to her. I speak of the maternal love as a representative of that love for another which is divorced from its lustful or selfish character—not based upon considerations of self-gain. We may desire the salvation of individuals on our own account, for our own enjoyment, and also from a love divorced from all considerations of self, which stands out holy, pure, and undefiled for a being outside of itself. The mother, in loving her child, experiences happiness; and as she presses it to her bosom, and imprints upon its delicate cheek the maternal kiss, there is joy deep and unutterable awakened in that mother's bosom; but she does not kiss the child that she may have the joy. It is not her joy and happiness that she seeks, but the comfort, happiness, and welfare of the child; and in thus supplying that demand of her maternal nature, she feels the influx of the divine nature, saying, "Well done, good and faithful servant; thou hast been faithful over a few things, I will make thee ruler over many things: enter into the joy of thy God." That is what God says to every mother who loves her babe from the true maternal feeling. So is it in the true relation between husband and wife. I mean now the union in heaven, and not the union fixed up by society and its institutions—I speak of such hearts as God has joined together. When the true husband meets the true wife and surrenders all his manhood to the care and keeping of that wife, in full confidence and trust that she will receive it and not abuse it; and when the wife in return gives all her womanhood to the care and fidelity of the trusting husband—when two such souls surrender each to each the other's self, loving from an interior and divine harmony, then the joys of conjugal love are awakened, the true demands of each soul are supplied in the experience of those joys which can be found alone in that relation, and God speaks saying, "Well done," and breathes his divine blessing upon them. So it is in the fraternal relation. Where from the natural, constitutional harmony of soul existing between brothers, each being individualized upon a common moral plane, and loving the other with a pure and undefiled love, their love belongs to the second sphere.

Where the individual loves his neighbor as himself, he would as soon sacrifice his own interest as that of his neighbor, and would as soon be unjust to himself, nay, sooner be unjust to himself, than to his neighbor. He loves that neighbor with a pure heart, loves him as a manifestation of his divine Father's Love, Will, and Wisdom, and seeks to harmonize his own being with him in all his relations. He can not see a brother, however weak, crushed, without seeing himself crushed in that brother. When he loves a brother with that pure, unselfish love—when the common heart of humanity abides in his breast, he comes into the true plane of charity; for charity is that which seeketh not her own. The motive that prompts him is not self-gain. It is the desire to do good unto others that actuates him. The quality of charity is to suffer long, not to be envious, not to be easily provoked, not to be puffed up, or behave itself unseemly; but in all things to be true and faithful, and kind to everybody. The man or woman possessed of this love, whose whole being and activity is directed in the sphere of relation to man, to society, to the world, belongs to what I call the second sphere, and gives evidence that he or she has risen above the lustful plane which seeketh its own, and which loves to gratify its passion, desires, and appetites, in one form or another, and that he or she is loving in harmony with God, and wills and acts in accordance with the divine impulses.

Look abroad into society, look at the love of the world, and see how many there are who love their neighbor with an unselfish love—how many are so careful to be exactly just with their neighbor as they are careful to have their neighbor be exactly just to them. There are many who watch the scale to see if it preponderates in their favor; and if the merchant gives good weight, they speak well of him; but if he does not give good weight, they are very ready to speak ill of him. When you come to see how much better they love to have justice done to them than they love to do justice to others, you have an indication that the lustful nature is somewhat alive and active in their breast. The individual who is conscious that his desire is earnestly to be just, will be as careful not to do an injustice to his neighbor as he would be cautious to avoid an injury to himself—will no sooner circulate defamatory remarks against his neighbor than he would defame himself. When you find an individual thus acting, you may be certain that he has risen from the first plane and is entering the second. But I am sorry to say that in the vast majority of cases you will find lust lamentably present. I called your attention to this in my last lecture, showing you how it was manifested in almost every sphere of life, even in performing the duties of a father, brother, husband, or wife. In the majority of cases man and society are loved for their uses.

When it is desired to ascertain whether we belong to the first or the second sphere—to the sphere of Gehenna or Paradise—we need only to determine the quality of the affection that rules in us, to see whether it be looking mainly to our own gain, or whether we rise above self and go out to seek the well-being of man. We sometimes mistake, thinking that we love a man himself, when we love his influence or society, because by it we think we can be elevated in our social condition. We ought, therefore, to be careful in trying ourselves to know to which plane of affection we belong, lest some of these considerations outside of the individual influence us, lest that we mistake for love that which, proved by the true standard, will appear to be selfishness and lust.

When one possesses a love for the well-being of all, he is willing to contribute liberally and freely of his strength and talent for the redemption of all, and has an unwillingness to be found at any time as the representative of that idea which would tend to degrade or crush any human being. There is no being so low in the scale of humanity as to be beneath his efforts to raise him up; and if the tyrant should stand upon the neck of the weak, his impulse is to push that tyrant off and break away the captive's chains, because he can not see his brother fettered without feeling fettered himself —can not see the humblest human being outlawed without seeing all humanity insulted. The individual who has not seen enough of the dignity of the nature of humanity to fulfill the duty he owes to universal humanity, has not yet come to the true plane of charity, is not qualified to occupy a high position in this second sphere.

I might illustrate in a variety of ways how it is that man apologizes to himself for being selfish. Here is a constitution, and there a law, and there a public sentiment demanding that a human being should be crushed; and he turns his back to humanity and God and bows to the Constitution. Such a man has not the love of humanity in his bosom; he loves that which is respectable and strong, and which may be of service to him under particular circumstances. But the individual who can be a Judas and can sell the Lord in the shape of his brother—can betray him with a kiss and sell him for thirty pieces of silver, whatever may be his profession—belongs to the lowest grade of humanity. Here is a truth that every soul must affirm. It honors the man that honors humanity, and despises the man that despises humanity.

When a man in his lustful nature will bring his whole soul to honor that sentiment, he is prepared to leave the first and enter the second sphere, which is expressive of the finite character of man as he comes into this charitable affection. This character in man is that which determines the second sphere in the world of Spirits. Man is a universe; and if there is a hell in the universe, it is because it is in man; and if there is a heaven, it is because there is a heaven in man. Those who are developed only in the sphere of outer darkness, and who from affinity love to associate together, will be found composing what is called the Outward Sphere. Do not now, by any means, associate the idea of sphere with that of place. The persons in this room are all together, so far as space is concerned, but so far as sentiment or sphere is concerned you may be at heaven-wide distances. While one is in *rapport* with celestial affections, holding communion with the Divine Father, the other may be in *rapport* with Spiritual beings, holding a communion with the angels; and a third may be in *rapport* with the infernal, holding communion with the spheres of lust. It is not a question of place, but simply a question of condition. If you and I are in the condition of lust in our affections and perceptions, if we associate with others in the same condition, heart thrills to heart, just as in the moral or divine sphere heart answers to heart. Each in his own plane seeks that which is adapted to his own nature. I say, therefore, do not connect the idea of place with that of sphere.

Man is a little universe—a microcosm. This sphere of lust is within him, from which the dark sphere of the Spiritual world is developed. Those who are in the sphere of lust on the earth respond to the inhabitants of this dark sphere of the Spiritual world. So also in the Spiritual spheres is the development of man's relational love. Man in fulfilling his relational duties lays the foundation of the Spiritual Paradise. Thus man rises and dwells in different spheres according to the development of his affections. If we love our neighbor as such, and seek after the redemption of man on his own account, we become allied to that band of guardian angels whose mission it is to watch over him and to stimulate in him impulses to resist that which is evil and impure. We become guardian angels, and every effort we put forth for the redemption of our fellow-man elevates our own souls. Hence the remark of the poet:

"Heart thrills to heart
Throughout the wide domain of heavenly life;
Each angel forms a chain which in God's throne begins,
And winds down to the lowest plane of earthly minds;
And only as each lifts his lower friend
Can each into superior joys ascend."

We are told that we must seek our salvation. That is bad advice. He that seeketh to save his life shall lose it. It is this very seeking to save ourselves that damns us and the race. It is the very selfish desire for salvation which allies us to the sphere of lust. The true spirit is to seek to save our fellow-man; and as we can not save him except by adapting our ideas to his needs, we must, as instruments to his salvation, put away our lust. That effort will result in our own salvation. There is but one way to save ourselves, and that is by fitting ourselves as the instruments for the redemption of the world. Laboring to redeem our outcast and down-trodden brother and sister is the very best kind of labor to elevate ourselves, since it exercises in us the true love for our fellow-men. Thus it appears that it is more blessed to give than to receive.

I may go out into the streets some cold morning, and seeing a beggar, stop and debate with myself whether he is worthy or not; or for fear that I may refuse the right one, I may drop a sixpence in his hand. From such an act I will not receive a blessing. But if I (in forgetfulness of considerations of that kind, from the overflowings of a loving heart, from a sincere desire to do good to a fellow-man who is in need) give him alms, it is laying up treasure in heaven. I have placed it at my Father's disposal—have intrusted it to one of his messengers.

We have a fashionable way of doing charities in this world. We do not like to be troubled with charities. We are willing to be taxed some—we are very generous to give sometimes; but then we do not want the trouble of finding the object, and bestowing it with that love, kindness, and sympathy of soul which carries more joy to the stricken heart than the poor pittance. He needs it as much as he does your other charities. But instead of taking this trouble, we raise contributions, appoint a committee, and go and drop our gifts by machinery here and there. If you will look up a poor sufferer some of these cold mornings, and give but a dime, with a blessing, you will not only carry joy into the heart of the suffering poor, but rejoicing into the Angel-spheres. In that way you must cast your bread upon the water, and you will find it after many days—will hear, eternally you will hear, the music of that poor sufferer's thankful heart. If you once in purity of soul, in the pure affection of your heart, go and bestow a kindness from a pure and fervent spirit, you will awaken a chord which will vibrate harmoniously in your soul to all eternity.

As man develops in himself a love of his fellow-man irrespective of exterior relation, but as a child of God, as possessing in his bosom the germ of immortality, and as endowed with a facility of eternal unfolding in the eternal future, he comes into the sphere of true charity; and when his work is faithfully done here, he will enter upon that reward which he has been laying up in heaven, where neither moth nor rust corrupts, and where thieves do not break through and steal.

There is between the first and second spheres, speaking of them in the affectional sense, another sphere, called the intellectual sphere. Man as an intellectual being has loves or delights. The quality of the intellect, you are aware, is to investigate, to think. Intellect of itself has no affection, no sympathy. It can be allied with vice or virtue. It can attend the missionary in his labor or the pirate in his murderous work. It has of itself no conscience, no moral quality. Hence you will find that men may be highly intellectual and vicious or virtuous. Intellect can join upon vice or crime, and upon charity and virtue, and that, too, without experiencing antagonism from such union. Man may be developed intellectually without affecting particularly his moral character. Intellect's particular mission is to investigate that which addresses the perception. It can join upon the sphere of lust or the sphere of charity. Were it not for this, the selfish and charitable natures could not unite in man, and there would be such an antagonism in the individual, he could not be possibly developed from the plane of his lustful nature to the plane of his moral nature. Intellect is a sort of John Baptist that goes between the Moses and the Christ of man's nature. It does not partake of the lust of Moses nor of the love of Christ. Its delights are sometimes mistaken for love, or the joys of love. People often say of things which are beautiful that they love them. They say that they *love* the study of mathematics. That expression seems to me to be improper. The heat of love is never known to the cold intellect. The intellect can discourse eloquently respecting justice and right; but, so far as the heart is concerned, it may trample upon all justice. You will see men who, so far as theory is concerned, will discourse eloquently concerning human justice and morality, yet they utterly disregard and ignore all moral restraints in their private character and practices. These men are babes in their moral natures —they are less than babes. Intellect has to do with the relations of things— pertains to dead matter. The difference between intellect and morals is the difference between the essence and spirit of matter and the essences or spirit of the soul. While science, which belongs to the province of intellect, may harmoniously journey with the moral affections, it may also journey with the sensuous affections. I make these remarks so that you may not suppose that a man belongs to the second sphere because of his having an intellectual character.

The second sphere is a finite one, and depends entirely upon relation for its development, so that you can see at once that man could not love in the second sphere of his being without some object to call that love forth. The relational love, in this respect, is not like the divine love which goes forth independent of any object. The first sphere is objective in self; the second sphere is objective in neighbor; and the third sphere is subjective in God.

The difference between this second sphere or love of the neighbor and the third sphere or the love of the absolute in this: The second sphere of love is objective, is not self-existent and self-sufficient; it depends upon having an object to call it forth. The constitution of mind is such that, in its consciousness, it can not love an object without having perceived it, the perception being either an ideal one or a real one. The love in point of quality depends, for its perfectness, upon the perfectness of the object. Not so with the infinite and divine love which is self-existent and self-sufficient. Wherever it acts, it acts subjectively, not objectively, though it is objective in its manifestation. Said Jesus of Nazareth, who was deeply learned in this love, in speaking to the Jew who was to become his disciple: "Ye have heard it said by those of old time, Thou shalt love thy neighbor and hate thine enemy; but I say unto you, Love your enemies, bless them that curse you, do good to them that hate you, and pray for them that despitefully use you; that you may be the children of your Father which is in heaven; for he causeth his sun to shine upon the evil and the good, and he sendeth his rain upon the just and unjust." Notice the figure. The sun shines not objectively. It shines of its own nature. If the earth were to be blotted out of existence, the sun would shine on still; and if every other planet in the solar system should refuse to receive its light, the sun would continue to shine. Its light and heat go forth in their own plenitude. Therefore if you and I wish the sunlight, we have but to stand forth; but the sun does not shine or send forth his heat because we are here. It does not shine objectively but subjectively upon us. The sun, as a type of the divine wisdom, continuously gives forth its light; and as a type of divine love it constantly gives forth heat to build up finite forms.

The Divine Father does not stop to inquire, whether men love him or not. His love is self-existent, self-sufficient, and goes forth of its own divine plenitude, of its own infinite fulness, blessing every being in every plane, according as he comes into the condition to receive that blessing. God's sun shines upon the field of the wicked man as quick as upon the field of the righteous. This is bestowing blessing upon a common plane. Man loves friend and curses foe, but Christ says you must not make any difference. You must become like your Father. You claim to be his children; therefore love your enemies, seek good for all, whatever may be their affection for you. Christ's doctrine differed very much from what the world had heard before. It had generally been supposed that God loved objectively. Christ taught that God blessed every man according to the plane he occupied. God of his infinite fulness will pour out all the blessings you are capable of receiving. If you want all the joys of the third heaven, which are inexpressible, bring your mind to love subjectively. Love God, not for his use, not because he is going to bless you, but because there is interior harmony and oneness between your soul and his—because your heart thrills and throbs to his divine heart. Then you will reap the blessings belonging to the divine plane. Man can only love an object by having an object to love; but God is love; it is his nature to love and bless; and whatever comes within the divine influence will be blessed according to its capacity to receive the blessing; and every action, every impulse, and every going forth of the divine in every plane is but a manifestation of that divine love; so that when you and I have perfected ourselves in loving our neighbor, have fulfilled the entire law of charity to all mankind, we are yet to go into a higher and holier love than that. We are to arise above this discrimination—we are to come into a plane where, having received the divine life and love, they shall go forth by their own plenitude to bless all around us, as our Father blesses all. In other words, he is to sit as a refiner and purifier of silver, and he is to purify us from all this dross, until he sees his own image perfectly reflected in us. When we shall reflect the divine image, there will be an indication that all dross is burned away, and we shall be swallowed up in the divine will, though still retaining our divine personality, our hearts beating with the great heart that beats throughout the universe.

CHAPTER IV.
COMMUNICATION.

Communication proper belongs to the sphere of manifestation, and signifies, as I use the term, the imparting by one, and the receiving by another, of that which is imparted, or that which represents that which is imparted. When we look at man as a finite being, born as he is without conscious knowledge, and without conscious affection, and developed from that negative point by that which flows or enters into his consciousness and daguerreotypes itself there, we readily see that he can only develop by being subject to the principles of communication: that is, he must receive that which is without into his consciousness; therefore it must be communicated to him. Hence it becomes necessary for us to understand somewhat the laws of communication. As communication belongs to the sphere of manifestation, or the sphere of the finite, we must examine and see what are the means by which man as a conscious being is addressed, and the law by which the influence exerted upon him is governed.

The mind when looked at in its simplest nature consists of its perceptions and its affections: that is, its knowledge, if you please, and its love; but in the order of unfolding, perception, as a conscious principle, precedes affection. That is, an individual as a finite being can not love till he perceives an object to call forth that love or affection. Whether it pertain to unconscious or to conscious nature, he must perceive the object before the affection is known to exist in his consciousness. For instance, a husband can know nothing of conjugal love, neither can the wife, until the object calling it forth exists in his or her perceptions. Neither can the mother love her babe until the object exists in her perceptions. Neither can the brother love brother or sister, or the child love its parents, until they perceive the objects of their affection. So you understand what I mean when I say in all finite natures perception precedes affection as a conscious principle; hence the law of communication pertains to perception and affection. As perception precedes affection, it is more external, view it in what sphere you will. I am now using perception in the sense of thought. The individual, by the means of communication, may be addressed externally by first addressing his perceptions, and thence through his perceptions addressing his affections; or he may be addressed by first addressing his affections, and through them his thoughts. I shall use for the purpose of convenience the expression thought and affection.

Then the two methods by which individuals may be addressed are first the external, and second the internal. The external communication flows first into the thought, and the internal first into the affection. The external proceeds from thought to affection, and the internal from affection to thought. The one is by an outward language, by signs, and symbols, and representatives of ideas; the other is without external language, and is what is known as inspiration.

Now, as there are three planes of conscious being, conscious perception, and conscious affection, and as the thought or perception precedes the affection in the first or lowest plane, so it is in the second; and it is the perception and affection in the third that begets the affection in the divine sphere. But as I am speaking of communication I am confining my remarks to the first two spheres—the external physical sphere, and the spiritual or relational sphere; for they are spheres of manifestation and communication, and have reference to these finite spheres. When I complete the consideration of these, I will make some remarks on the divine sphere, to show the difference between it and those spheres below the divine. Take man, then, as a mere animal being, looking at his nature as being nervous, where his perceptions and affections have respect to his physical being. Here the same law of order prevails—perception precedes affection, and perception is external, while affection or love is internal; but taken both together as constituting the animal nature, it becomes external to his spiritual nature; but in his spiritual nature perception precedes affection; hence, if we would communicate with him spiritually, external language communicates first with thought, and thence with the affection; while internal language communicates first with the affection and thence with thought. Then external and internal communication differ in this, that the external is by means of outward language, and the internal is by means of a sort of inspiration. There are inspirations pertaining to each of the three spheres—the nerve-sphere, the spirit-sphere, and the divine-sphere. On coming into *rapport* with this audience, I through the nerve-medium by external means perceive individuals about me—perceive their forms, their faces, and their relative positions to each other; that is, by an external medium which represents the individual through the nerve-medium to my consciousness. But I may come internally into *rapport* with these individuals by bringing my nerve-system into harmony with their nerve-system, and becoming negative to them. To explain: when I bring my nerve-system into sympathy with you, I take your sensations upon myself. If you have a pain in your head, I have a pain in my head also, corresponding in location and character to yours; or if you experience a pain in any other part of your body, I feel that pain. Not a word has passed between us concerning it, but nevertheless it comes upon me, and affects me in precisely the same manner that it does you. Now this I consider analogous to the inspiration which belongs to the higher plane. This is the inspiration of the nerve-sympathy. Permit me to explain briefly what I understand by harmony; because the great law of harmony is fundamental to a comprehension of the law of inspiration.

You are aware that if we take two strings of equal length and tension, and vibrate one of them, its vibration communicates its motion to the atmosphere, and through the atmosphere to the adjoining string, so that they at length vibrate together. This experiment may be made by any one; and it will be found that in this manner they can be caused to give forth the same sound, because the length of the vibrations of each will be the same; and when there is a difference in the tone, it will be found that there is a difference in the length of the vibrations. This fact can be demonstrated by varying the vibrations—by tightening or loosening the strings, and thus shortening or lengthening the vibrations, when it will be perceived that the shorter the vibration the higher will be the pitch or tone. The length of vibration, then, determines the question of harmony. Here appears the great law of harmony in musical sound throughout the universe, which is commensurability. In mathematics, things which will mutually measure each other are said to be commensurable. Now these spheres of atmospheric vibration will always produce concord or harmony of sound. The difference between a third and a fifth is in the difference in the tone, and the difference in tone depends, as already said, upon the length of vibration. The sweetest harmony is the apparent discord, where the vibrations do not chord, but where every fifth coincides; and in this way produces the harmony of the third and fifth. The octave produces it by being repeated twice, so that after all the real octave is as the square of the octave; that is, the octave multiplied into itself; and you arrive mathematically at the law of harmony by following out that principle. The point to which I wish to call your attention is, that what constitutes harmony is simply commensurability in the atmospheric undulations.

Now my nerve-fluid moves by pulsatory movements, as move all other media, and these movements sustain to those of your nerve-fluid commensurable or incommensurable relations; and you will find that the law of musical harmony, by which one of two strings having the same tension communicates its motion to the other, is the law which determines the harmony between my nerve-system and yours. I am constituted to speak upon a certain key, like an instrument. My nerve-vibrations undulate to that key, and when I am in perfect health, there is perfect harmony in my system. Your nerve-undulations are perhaps tuned on a different key, and if you are positive to me, my nerve-undulation will not move yours, nor yours mine, but they will resist each other like two strings unequally tuned. So my nerve-vibration will not communicate its undulations to you, nor will yours communicate its undulations to me, unless we happen to be upon the same key, or in harmonic or commensurable relations with one another. But in order to get our nerve-systems to undulate one upon the other, I must either become negative to you or you must become negative to me. If I relax the key of my nerve-vibration, I shall change them until my nerve-system undulates in harmony with your nerve-system; and I being negative and you positive, you undulate to my key, and we get nerve-sensations between us without any sign. The individual in mesmerizing his subject becomes positive, and he will succeed in mesmerizing that subject just as soon as he brings about a harmony of nerve-vibration, so that the nerve-vibrations of both are alike. The condition is that the operator places himself in a positive position, while the subject must become negative, by allowing his nerves to become relaxed; then the operator commences by a strong effort to undulate, so to speak, his nerve-influence or forces upon the medium, until the medium sinking down comes to his key; and then he by his forces insulates the system, and the individual passes rapidly into the condition of mesmerism; but do any thing to disturb that medium, so as to make the points of nerve-tension unyielding, and the operator may work till doomsday in vain. It is not till the points have yielded and the vibrations harmonize with his that he can produce the effect upon the medium. This is on the same principle with the phenomena exhibited in experiments with the string, which is a type of the law of communication in every sphere— the vibration of the string represents the entire law.

Take one string whose points of tension are unyielding, and another whose points of tension are yielding; then cause one of them to undulate, and it will impart its motion to the atmosphere, when the atmosphere will strike upon the other; and if it have the same points of tension that the other has, it will undulate; but if it have not the same tension, it will receive the influence of the atmosphere, the tendency of which will be to depress it and bring it to its own vibration; thus eventually the two strings will be made to harmonize. So when we sit down to mesmerize a person, he may be so positive that we do not at first succeed, perhaps, in producing the least impression upon him. We try again and again, and at last succeed in controlling the nerve-system, and through that the mental system of the subject. We are each time we try reducing the nerve-system to our key or standard, and the moment it is reduced to that point, the subject is under the operator's control, and not till then. When I speak of the harmonic action of one system upon another, it will be perceived that I speak of the relative measure or length of the nerve-undulation which passes between one mind and another. In the nerve-plane there is this method of addressing the nervous perceptions by external means—by language, by signs, by pantomimic representations. And there is the internal method corresponding to inspiration, which consists in coming into nervous sympathy and receiving nervous sensations one from another. A sensitive person looking upon a wound shrinks from beholding the sight, and there are real sensations experienced in his nervous system which have been produced, not because a nerve-influence has acted upon him, but because he has seen the wound. The impression first fell upon his conscious perceptions, and then went to his feelings, which is analogous to the principle that the idea first comes into the thought, and thence reaches the feelings.

In the second plane—the mental or Spiritual plane—the same law prevails. There is the external method of addressing the mind, and there is also an internal method. The external is the method by which the mind is addressed first through the thought, and the internal is that by which the mind is addressed through the feelings. These two methods obtain in the whole plane of manifestation. If I wish to communicate with you, I must adopt one of these two methods; and if I am not in spiritual or nervous *rapport* with you, I must adopt one of the methods of external communication, and address you by signs or outward representations—addressing first the thought or understanding, and coming thence to the affection indirectly. In all external methods, as well as in internal methods, media of communication become necessary. In speaking to you it becomes necessary that there should be some external media between you and me, and my communication must be through that media. In the present case, my speaking to you is performed through the physical atmosphere. I undulate my organs of speech to produce sound, and the atmosphere connects them with your organs of hearing, so that my mind, through my organs of speech, is connected with your mind. The method of communication is to transmit the actions of my organs of speech to your organs of hearing. Without this external medium I could not communicate with you by an external language.

Were I to address, not the ear, but the eye, there must be between us an external medium which addresses the eye; and that medium is the light which takes up the image of that which I would represent, and transmits it to your consciousness through the eye. So also in respect to the nerve-medium. If I would communicate an impression through the nerve-medium, there must be that medium external to me which corresponds to the action of the nerve-fluid in you and me—there must be a medium between us which takes up my action and transmits it to you, and makes it your action. So with the mental medium. If I am to stand here, and you are to come into *rapport* with me, and I am to impress my thoughts upon you without external language, there must be a medium corresponding to these thoughts, and that medium must come down from me to you; and while I have power to awaken its vibration, its vibration must have power to awaken the same impression in you. Hence, then, in respect to all communication, there must necessarily be media connecting one with the other, who are all concerned in making and receiving the communication; and the medium must be such that it will extend from the one to the other. It must be continuous also; for if there be any interruption in the media, the communication can not be transmitted. For illustration, if I would address your consciousness through sound, the atmosphere, as the medium, must be continuous between you and me; for if you interpose a vacuum, you can not transmit the action through it, the connection being destroyed. So in regard to light. Interpose any medium which will not allow the light to pass through it, and I can not transmit the image by means of light. So also the nerve-medium must be continuous, in order to admit of transmitting communication through it. The mental medium must likewise be continuous, or I can not represent my thought through it. You perceive, then, this universal law in respect to communication between one mind and another, that there must necessarily intervene a medium, which must be continuous between them, and it must be such as to awaken action in the one, and transmit and awaken the same action in the other. It matters not what the plane is. They all come under the same law.

Before I, by my simple will-power, can transmit a thought or idea or impression of my mind to you, there must be something between us which can take up and repeat that idea, or record it in your consciousness. If there be anything to interrupt this medium, I can not transmit that thought; so that any power whatever which can interrupt that medium can interrupt the communication. Hence, again, it appears that in all communication between one being and another, there must necessarily interpose a medium, which must be continuous from the communicator to the one receiving the communication. This brings us to the consideration of other conditions necessary for communication between two minds—the difference between the thing, the being, or the existence itself, and that by which it is made known to the mind. I stand here before you. You can see me. I am then present in each one of your minds. I am present by my form, as well as by the sound of my voice. How many of me are there here? One, of course. How many do you see? How many of my mental images are here? Just as many as there are eyes to look. My image is that by which you see me. My image is not in your mind in reality; it is represented in your mind by something proceeding from me to you. My form is multiplied and repeated wherever there is an eye to see the image which proceeds from this form. If there are two or three hundred persons present, I have two or three hundred spiritual forms; and if there were ten thousand present, I should have ten thousand spiritual forms. There is a difference, then, between the form itself and that which represents the form, and you should make this distinction.

You may take as many positions as there are mathematical points in this room, and place an eye in each, and my form will be represented in all of these points. The means, then, by which you, through the eye, become conscious of my presence here, is omnipresent in this room. I am not omnipresent, but that which represents me is omnipresent, and that by which mind becomes conscious of me is omnipresent.

There is never any existence to the mind in the sphere of manifestation, except by representation. We talk as though we saw the sun, moon, and stars, and not as though we saw their representations; but in regard to all things external or manifestational, man in all forms only perceives the representation; and when the representation corresponds to the reality, he has the truth. Now in looking at these lights, the light is not in your mind, but its representation is there. It is there by that which represents it. Then you must make a distinction between the omnipresence of being and of that which represents being. In respect to all means by which the mind perceives existence external to its consciousness, it is true that it only perceives it by representation, and not by its presence. Existence in every department is represented to your mind, and mind by its representation, and not by its absolute presence, perceives it. Understand this distinction, and it will explain a great many mysteries you have had to contend with in times past. As you perceive my form by that which represents it to you, and as that which represents it is omnipresent in this room, while my form, from which these representations flow, has but one position, so also, if you should remove these walls many feet, or even miles, making this room many miles in extent, my form would be omnipresent in all this space, and the mind that perceived me would perceive me by that representation of form, and not by my presence.

Now then, understanding this law, we will be very careful in all our investigations of communication to distinguish between the presence of the thing itself and the presence of that which represents it. Did I wish to communicate with a Spirit, who has unfolded in him a Spirit-consciousness, which can be addressed in another way than through the physical eye or ear or touch, and being so divested of this physical form that my mind comes in absolute contact with this Spirit-medium which permeates all space, and which internally and spiritually corresponds to light external and physical, and passes freely through bodies opaque to light—then my Spirit-form acts upon that Spirit-medium which is not impeded by this wall, but which passes through it as light through transparent glass, carrying my image with it. We say that glass is transparent, because light passes freely through it, and brings the image of that which it would represent. We see an individual or tree coming freely through the glass into the room. Now if we have a medium which will pass as freely through a board, then that board is as transparent to that medium as glass is to light. The magnetic medium, by which the magnetic needle is influenced, passes freely through a board even; therefore to that medium the board is as transparent as glass is to light. It is also well to understand that this nerve-medium, as well as the spiritual medium corresponding to the mind—which is to the mind what the medium of light is to the eye—passes freely through these opaque bodies. Therefore the individual brought in contact with this medium will see Spirit-existences, not by their presence in the consciousness, but by that which represents the presence there. Hence it is that the clairvoyant (when you have proceeded with your manipulation until you have insulated the mind, or brought it into clear *rapport* with this spiritual medium or atmosphere so that he sees by the spiritual sight and hears with the spiritual ear, and no longer sees with the physical eye, or hears with the physical ear) comes in contact with this spiritual medium, and can look out into another room, and tell what is transpiring, who is there, etc., just as we can look through glass and tell what we see. The principle is precisely the same. The medium by which he perceives things in another room freely permeates or passes through the intervening walls; so that although my spiritual form is still in this body, yet it is actually exerting its influence on this spiritual medium throughout the world—throughout not only this world, but throughout the solar system. Wherever this spiritual medium extends, this spiritual image of mine is taken and carried out through that medium, just as my physical image is carried out through the medium of light; and whoever comes into *rapport* with that Spirit-medium and influence, and undulates to the same motion, will perceive that form. Hence coming into the clairvoyant condition I may see a person in London, if it so happen that the undulation of my mind on this medium be such as to harmonize with that of the individual in London—not that his spirit is personally here present, or my spirit personally present there (but I am here in my own spirit-consciousness, and he there in his spirit-consciousness), but because his image as well as mine is here and there and everywhere else. The idea that my mind goes to London, or his comes here, is altogether a misconception. I perceive that individual in London, not by his absolute presence, but by that which represents that presence here; just as I see you, not by your presence in my mind, but by that which represents your presence there. It is in this way that persons in the body are at times seen as though in distant places; that is, they are seen by that spiritual image which is present, where the mind is unfolded so as to perceive by the spiritual medium, and happens to be in *rapport* so as to undulate to the same motion with that of the mind of the individual it perceives.

Standing here this evening, I may be seen in Philadelphia, because my image is there, as well as in every other place on earth; and the individual, let him be where he may, who happens to be in *rapport* with me, will perceive me as though I were present where he is, and all the imagery by which I am surrounded. I am looking on this congregation, and therefore the person seeing me, sees me surrounded by this congregation. He does not see you, but since you are in my mind, your image goes with mine. The person coming into *rapport* with me, sees you as your image exists in my mind. The idea that persons whose external forms are in different places, communicate with each other by being present one with the other, is altogether a mistaken one. So far as the external or relational is concerned—so far as the finite or manifestational is concerned—we communicate externally only by that medium which represents that which we investigate or perceive; and that is the peculiarity of arriving at knowledge through what is called the sphere of manifestation. The difference between being and manifestation is seen in that law.

If any one doubts this law, I am ready to be questioned. Bring up any case you please, either from the natural or the Spiritual world, and I will show that that is the law. I say it is altogether a fallacious idea that Spirits can not communicate without being actually present—the idea that Spirits can not communicate in New York, London, Liverpool, or any other place in the world at the same moment, is altogether a fallacious idea. They can be present wherever there is a mind in *rapport* with them to see that presence. People talk about their being so rapid in their passage from here to Boston or London, and wonder how they can go over the ground so quick. This is all explained when you understand the law of manifestation. There is no apparent difference of time between London and any other place—it is only a relative difference—merely a question of relation. This, then, being the law of communication and manifestation, we will just notice one thing further, which will explain why it is that individuals are obliged to come into certain states to receive communications, and will answer many other questions, among which are, "Why are not all mediums?" "Why can not all get communications?" "Why is it that one who can get a communication at one time can not at another?" Ten thousand such questions are pressed every day, when the law is just as simple as that two and two make four.

If we wish to get a communication we must conform to the conditions required by the law; and if we do not conform to those conditions, God himself could not give it to us. The laws of manifestation and communication are as fixed and immutable as God's own being. Our business is to comply with the conditions, and then take what follows. We need not stop to quarrel because it requires a wire rather than a tow-string to make a good telegraph. It is enough for us to know that it is so, and conform to the conditions.

The great law by which all action producing result, producing development and communication, is governed, is the one to which I first referred—the law of commensurability in form and motion. All development comes under that law. The law of triunes, the law of sevens, and the law of twelves, are all wrought out by that simple law. You can not develop in any key except you comply with that law. Commensurability tends to produce harmonious results, while incommensurability tends to produce discord and death—the difference between concord and discord marks the difference between commensurability and incommensurability in form and motion.

We have several different departments of our systems, I have a vital, a nervous, and a mental system, each of which has actions peculiar to itself—actions which sustain to each other certain relations, either commensurable or incommensurable. Now, when my spiritual and vital systems act upon the same key, there is harmony between my internal and external forms; but if they do not undulate to the same key—if there is not harmonious action between my mind and spirit, I can not be a medium for physical communication, for the same reason that if you graft a peach upon an apple, you can not make it grow (according to my information). It is because the vital action between them is an incommensurable action. Now, whenever my mental action is too intense for my nerve or vital action, if you will by any means reduce my mental action so that it may harmonize with my nervous action, perhaps I will get physical manifestations peculiar to myself. I was once one of those things called mediums, and am now, perhaps, to some extent. When I was partially asleep there would be very loud raps, and if you could come in without waking me up you might get a communication, and it has ever been so when I am peculiarly quiet mentally; but the moment I rouse up and ask questions I can get no reply. There are others who require exactly opposite conditions, whose bodies are too active for their minds, in whose presence you can get rappings by reducing the action of the body. But you change them from that point, the manifestation ceases. There are other individuals who in the normal state seem to comply with all the conditions necessary; that is, whose vital and nervous actions are the same; but you make them angry or stir up within them feelings of dread or fear, and your manifestations cease, simply because there is no harmonic action between the mental and physical systems.

Persons boast, at times, of being able to destroy the power of mediums; but nothing could be simpler, for a powerful battery may have its action stopped by lifting out the connecting wire, simply by disarranging the conditions of its action. It is often the case that the entrance of a person into a circle where manifestations are occurring, causes their discontinuance, and the person is perhaps astonished to think the Spirits should be so contrary. It was simply because he had come in and violated the conditions by which they could manifest. He had, so to speak, disturbed one of the plates of the battery. The law to which your attention is called, is this great law of commensurability in form and motion; or, in other words, the law of harmonic action, which is manifested not only in the material plane, but unfolded in every degree upon the conscious plane. In consequence of this law the communication between spheres differing in their characteristics must necessarily be external; that is, I can not communicate with an individual by the internal method, or the method of inspiration, except he is on the same plane with myself. Perhaps there is not one individual here so exactly on the same nerve-plane with myself, that I could communicate with him without signs; yet I can reveal my form so that you can all see me, by an external method, though we belong, perhaps, to very different planes. We can all communicate by external language, provided in our communications, we take that plane of communication which will be familiar to all present. This is the law existing between minds out of the physical body. One mind out of the physical body may communicate with another out of the physical body, by an external means, when he can not by the internal. The external means does not come directly to the affection. The vulgar and the profane man may speak to the refined mind by means of speech so as to shock the feelings; but he can not speak by his sympathy.

One class of individuals in the sphere of lust—in what we call the low and polluted plane—can not come into *rapport* with those occupying a higher plane. There is an "impassable gulf" between them. Nevertheless, by the external language which addresses the external being, the thought or perception, they may be able to communicate. The same law of communication applies in the Spiritual world. If angels are employed as messengers, they communicate by an external language; because their thoughts can not flow into the lower affection—the lower can not respond to them. If a Spirit in Paradise wishes to communicate with one in the sphere of lust, he must take upon himself the conditions of lust, or he can not communicate by the internal method. He can not communicate by the internal method, because the conditions are dissimilar. Communications made to us from a higher plane must be external, and must be addressed to our thought; and if they operate upon our affection, must flow from the thought into the affection. It is for this reason that God, the Divine, can not communicate with man, the imperfect and finite, except by means of those who can receive truth from the Divine, and who can externally communicate it to those below.

Spirits under a higher and more perfect law can not come and inspire us in our polluted condition, but they can, by means of external language, draw us from our low condition of lust, and bring us to a plane where a Spirit nearer to our plane may by influx come into us and develop within us the true affection; but the high spirit can not do it. Hence it is that there is a gradation between the highest and lowest—that

"Angels form a chain which in God's burning throne begins, And winds down to the lowest plane of earthly things."

I may possibly receive a communication from a higher plane by abstracting myself from the lusts and evils of the world, by sending forth my highest, and holiest, and purest aspirations after all that is pure and good —for a moment elevating my condition to a higher plane. That is the condition of true prayer. While in that condition a Spirit of that higher plane may, by influx, raise me up and hold me in that condition. That is, the true effect of the condition known as prayer, is to separate you from the lusts and passions of the world—every thing which is tending to degrade you. Then by fixing your mind on your highest perception, and that which is pure, and true, and holy, you elevate yourself above the plane on which you naturally move—bring yourself where a higher angel can reach down and raise you up. Therefore, though prayer does not change the state of the soul, yet it is one of the conditions by which we climb to the higher spheres. You know the direction in regard to prayer was, "when you pray do not go into the public places and talk a great deal, thinking God is going to hear you for your much speaking."

The object of prayer is not to inform God—to change his mind— therefore when you pray, retire from the world and all outward influences, and if necessary go into a room, and shut the world out with all its influences; and then, in the secret aspirations of your soul, raise your thoughts and desires to the infinite, perfect, and undying, that you may bring yourself within the plane of blessing—within the plane of that influence which can elevate you. If God could come down to our plane, and by the influx of his Spirit into our consciousness could enlighten our understandings and purify our hearts, there is no excuse for its not being done. He is infinite, and there is an infinite fullness in him; but the reason he does not, is that he can not. It is impossible that God should lie, and it would be lying if he should do this.

Conditions can not be at the same time unlike and like—at the same time discordant and harmonious; the plane of lust can not harmonize with the plane of love. The plane of man in his low condition can not harmonize with the plane of the Divine in his infinitely elevated, pure, and holy condition. Therefore if a man would receive God into his consciousness, he must put himself into the condition to receive influx; and if he would have an influx from a pure Spirit, he must become pure and holy himself. If God did not teach Moses so that he could understand all truth, as did the Man of Nazareth, and understand the great principle, "Thou shalt not resist evil by evil," it was because he did not occupy the plane of inspiration. He occupied a plane where there could be external manifestations, which he had, but he could not receive a great universal law, because he was not on the plane of the internal and divine. The inspiration of Paul, Peter, Luke, and John, was not equal to that of their Teacher, because they had not arisen to his elevated condition; had they occupied his plane, God could have communicated as well to them as to their Teacher; and it would not have been necessary for them to have a middle-man to come between them and God.

When you have risen to the plane of communication, the communication is internal. You have no outward form of expression, because you have the thought itself by inspiration. In the language of the Apostle, God writes his language in your understanding and in your affections. All communication with the spiritual world proceeding according to this law, each man's communication will be according to his plane; if in the low plane of lust, his communications will be of that character; if in the plane of love, his communications will be of that character. But even the lowest, by putting himself in the condition of prayer, by aspiring for the good and the holy, by putting up earnest petitions for aid, will always find a Spirit near to sustain and elevate him.

CHAPTER V.
PHILOSOPHY OF PROGRESSION.

If we wish to arrive at an accurate knowledge of any subject, we must endeavor to ascertain what is fundamental to that subject. If we need to investigate accurately any science, we need to inform ourselves as early as possible of the fundamental principles pertaining to that science. There is no better way to study the history of creation than by studying it as revealed in the phenomena of Nature. When I can investigate Nature in her operations, and ascertain the laws by which she performs her work, I then can arrive—at least approximately—at the philosophy of Nature, in attaining which I attain the philosophy of divine manifestation. There can be no interpolation there. The Divine Artificer works alone in the fields of Nature, and where I can discover the manifestation of wisdom and power, there I come directly into communication with the Divine Being in that plane of action and manifestation; and when I learn what the law of action and manifestation is in that department, I learn so much of the method of the divine work, or of the divine order. I propose, then, briefly to call your attention to the teachings of God upon this subject of progression, as manifested in the fields of Nature; and will then ask you to accompany me in endeavoring to ascertain what are some of its fundamental laws.

Were I to inquire what is the apparent design of everything we behold, we must see that it is pointing to the ultimating of an individualized, immortal, intelligent being, who should be capable of understanding all truth, and being perfected in every true affection. Everything tends to bring about that great result—the unfolding of an immortal being. God and the material universe seem to be laboring to beget an individualized being in the image of both God and the universe—God as the absolute and infinite, and matter as the finite, uniting, produce a being which partakes of both the absolute or infinite and the finite. When viewed from one plane he is infinite; when viewed from another plane he is finite; so that between God and matter man is mediate. I would say, then, in simple language, God is the father of the spirit, and matter the mother of his form. The first step in the path of unfolding, as taught by Nature, is that of individualizing form. The next step is that of individualizing life, of producing individuality. The last step is that of producing personality, making the individual a personal being. The form is necessarily finite. The mind can conceive of it only as finite, and as composed of that which is the absolute, finite matter, which, separate from the divine being, has no life or power. It is not self-sufficient nor conscious.

If we can suppose that matter shall be divested from all connection with media which can impress upon it a condition, we speak of it as being amorphous matter, or matter without form. If we unite it then with one medium, as electricity, we find it tending to produce the gaseous condition, the nebular condition. Form is not yet attained. If we unite with it still another medium which is a little different from electricity, forms of the mineral kingdom are produced. We have here the first degree of form, but as yet there is not life or individuality. Now the next advance is to induce in that form a condition which shall make it receptive of life, for that which is to be individualized is life. So, then, in passing through the elaborating influences of the mineral kingdom, it arrives at a certain point, a sort of culminating point, where it joins upon the vegetable kingdom; and the line between these kingdoms is passed by such imperceptible gradations—so slow in the unfolding of forms—that it is impossible for the naturalist to tell accurately where the one begins and where the other ends; but the vegetable kingdom is manifestly begun when there is found the incorporation of a new principle into a new form—a principle looking to organization—giving matter an organic structure. When the principle known as the life-force is introduced, then it is understood that mineral has passed and the vegetable is commenced. As soon as this is unfolded, we have a second advance of form—life in its first degree; or, in other words, individualization commences. Form has passed to its second degree, and goes on elaborating degree after degree, producing diverse organic forms, until it is prepared to receive another and a more interior principle—consciousness—until by imperceptible degrees we arrive at the animal kingdom. We have then the animal form, the third or finishing degree of form, and the second degree of life, and the first degree of consciousness. Man in his animal nature is the completion; of the highest form. Life has yet one more degree to pass through; consciousness has yet two more degrees to pass through before it is complete. The next advance is to a higher principle of consciousness—to a more enduring principle of life, without changing the material form, and that is to the spiritual degree of unfolding.

Looking to the highest types of the animal and the lowest types of men, we will observe that they approach very near to each other. Naturalists have been divided in opinion as to whether or not man was an animal projected on a little higher plane, and whether or not the difference is not merely one of degree. I say that when man is developed, we find him developing or individualizing a higher principle. Individuality was first started in the vegetable; the principle of vitality in the animal. The second degree of individuality was where the animal became individualized on a higher plane of life, on a plane of consciousness belonging to what we call the nerve-medium. Man individualizes upon the second degree of consciousness and the third degree of life, completing an individuality. He becomes to us the highest type of form and life in the finite; and a large class of philosophers and theologians conceive man as formed in the divine image, and suppose the expression that God made man in his own image, to refer to an external as well as internal likeness.

Man as an individual occupies the highest plane; he has attained to the third degree of life as a Spiritual being, consequently he becomes immortal. If the third degree of life brings man into communion with the self-living and divine, he becomes immortal; if not, then he is not immortal; for that only is immortal which receives into itself that which is self-living, self-sufficient, and self-existent, that which can not be dissolved or disorganized. If man has not attained to that plane which joins upon that which is self-existent, he is not immortal. The simple fact that man can think, will, and act, proves nothing for his immortality. The dog can act, and think, and will, but that does not make the animal immortal. Those who base immortality upon that, do not perceive its real basis. Man becomes immortal by his *relation* to that which is self-existent and self-sufficient, and has that self-sufficient condition brought into him by induction. He receives it by a sort of divine induction. I have brought in a chart to illustrate the principle of induction or the law of progression. You observe that man stands at the head of form and life, though not at the head of consciousness. He is as a finite being produced only to the second degree of consciousness. That is the last step man took. Man has advanced to the second degree of consciousness, which looks to the relational and finite, hence man as a moral being, as a finite being; and that which he investigates in virtue of his faculties as a moral being must be finite. He can therefore only investigate in the sphere of the finite. The moment he attempts to embrace the infinite, and translate that into the finite, that moment he is pushing his investigations beyond his development.

But there is not only this second degree of consciousness, which notices the relation, but there is a third degree, which notices or perceives the absolute. It perceives not only outward form and mediate relation, but the absolute essence of all being. Man attains to that, not because that third nature is individualized in him, but because by reason of its conjunction upon that condition which is known as the absolute, he has that condition in him by a sort of induction—a non-individualized condition, a sort of resident divinity in him, gives him this third degree.

Now permit me to illustrate the principle of induction. You understand, when electric conditions are produced, that there is such a thing as causing them by induction. You understand that negative attracts positive, and that positive attracts negative—that where these opposite conditions prevail there is a tendency to bring them together. Similar conditions repel, and opposite conditions attract, each other. We understand that all electrical currents are double—that there is a primary and a secondary current. In vitality, in nerve-aura, in whatever acts as a medium, there is a double current. The second current is within the primary, and runs in the opposite direction. It is more interior than the primary. Now, if I have a body charged positively, and I bring it into a certain relation to another body, it imparts its electricity to it. This is called producing the condition by induction. I speak now of progression under this law of induction.

Suppose, now, that we take the two great principles of life—consciousness and action on the one hand, and death, unconsciousness, or inertia on the other hand—one being impartive and the other negative and receptive. God on the one hand and matter on the other. (Pardon me for speaking of God as a principle, the subject requires it. Whatever is attempted to be explained in language must necessarily be considered as finite.) Now, whatever pertains to the divine and absolute on the one hand, the very opposite pertains to matter on the other hand; hence we speak of the sufficiency of Deity and the inertia of matter. This principle of inertia, however, is as essential to the development of form and individuality in the finite as the principle of consciousness is to the conscious being. Without the two conditions, that which is mediate could not be elaborated or produced. God's creative agency, the positive current, passes out upon matter, from which there is a current returning to mind, in which negative current individualization takes place. The returning current first begins to elaborate form; next, with the progress of matter, comes individuality; next, personality. The formative principle is in the secondary current, which produces induction; but that which is interior to form and elaborates it is the induced or positive current, which partakes of the positive or energetic action of the divine current, so to speak. In this way, by induction, form after form is elaborated and made to become the receptive of certain conditions. Matter has no power of itself, but at the same time is receptive of influences or conditions.

Two theories have prevailed respecting the origin of man. One is what we call the theory of supernaturalism, which supposes that the divine being, at a certain period of time, when every other condition was fulfilled, came down, and by special power formed man in his present shape, and imparted to him his present spiritual life; and that from that man thus formed, and a woman formed for his companion, sprang all the rest of the human family. Others, who adhere to this idea in general, suppose that there was a plurality of parents, from whom the human race have proceeded. The opposite theory is, that man has been developed from the animal kingdom—that he is a development of the animal in a higher plane. This theory was advocated by La Marc. Now, I believe in neither theory. The truth lies between the two. In the outset I made this remark, which I intended to be understood as meaning all that it implied: that God is the Father of the spirit, while matter is the mother of the form. Matter is finite in all its attributes and qualities. God is infinite in all his attributes and qualities. Man is taken from the finite in his lower plane. His form is nourished and fed by its connection with the finite, and when the spirit is separated therefrom, this portion of man goes to decay; and so far as he is concerned as an individual, he is no more. On the other hand, man comes from the infinite, in the higher department of his being, so that man partakes of both the finite and the infinite. He is in the image of his mother, as well as of his father. He is created in the image of

God and the image of matter. He has both an individuality and a personality. In his finity he is an individual; in his divinity he is personal. Therefore man contains in himself all the germinal elements of the universe, and also the representative elements of the Divine Being.

As a being of form man became receptive of conditions. The mineral eventually became receptive of the principle of life, which developed the vegetable kingdom. The moment this life-principle began to work in producing organic structure and multiplying relations and conditions, a variety of forms succeeded, until forms were brought to such a point that they became receptive of a higher principle—the nerve principle or consciousness, and the animal kingdom was the result. The vegetable kingdom only produced the form. The spirit came into it by induction from the other direction. The vegetable did not produce the animal; it merely produced the conditions by which this conscious principle could be induced into the individuality developed by the vegetable. That individuality was raised out of the vegetable and placed upon the animal plane, and a new kingdom was born by the application of the law of commensurability. Eventually form was elaborated through the entire animal kingdom until the highest form the nerve-principle could produce, was produced.

The human form was elaborated through the animal kingdom, but the spirit was not elaborated there. When the nerve-principle had done its best, had fulfilled its highest possible condition, and had brought form to join upon spirit, the condition of spirit was induced into this form; and the induction of that spirit raised the form of the animal kingdom into the human kingdom; and the first man thus stood forth, produced by the divine breath breathing into him, consequently the difference between the lowest man and the highest animal was very slight. The man, to be sure, takes his animal body, appetites, senses, and the laws which govern in the development of his body, from the animal, but not that which pertained to his spiritual, nature. It received this from above by the induction of the divine principle which took hold of the form and raised him out of the animal kingdom; so that man does not trace his parentage to the animal but to God. He has been begotten by the spirit and power of God, operating through every plane of being and action from the crystal to the divine. I detract nothing from the divine wisdom and power when I say that God works in an orderly and methodic manner. Forms are of the earth, but the spirit is from heaven. The first man is of the earth, earthy; the second man is the lord from heaven.

Every operation on the material side of the universe looks to the ultimating of a form which shall be so perfect as to become receptive of a spirit which shall be capable of living forever, of being conscious of all that is, of being truly affected by that which it perceives. There is not an operation in nature, not even the progress of the comet in its path, which does not look to the production of a human being, the production of an immortal soul. There is not a manifestation of power or wisdom in the world which is not laboring and conspiring to accomplish this great end of producing a son, a child of God, which shall be capacitated to be receptive of its divine origin. We shall eventually see that every law which we now think is working for destruction, is but the going forth of the divine power to produce the being, man.

I said that man was not immortal in consequence of his spirit-individuality alone. The reason that man is immortal is very manifest. The highest principle in the animal individuality is the nerve-principle, the principle of consciousness which can perceive material forms and material phenomena. That interior principle is not unfolded in the animal. The inmost principle of the animal, I grant, is spiritual, but that principle is not individualized. The animal has only the nerve-principle, but in the spirit-principle; and joining perceive facts and phenomena; but he can not perceive relations—has no desire after relations—and knows nothing of moral duties. He can not be active in that way, because his highest individuality is his mere nervous individuality. God does not breathe into the animal that breath of life which makes him a living soul. But man is individualized not only in this nerve-principle, but in the spirit-principle; and joining upon the infinite he does take the divine breath into him as the inmost principle of his being. Man is immortal by his relation to the self-sufficient and self-existent. It is his *relation* to God that makes him immortal. The animal is not immortal, because he has not this relation. Man having this higher principle individualized in him becomes a religious being.

In the example heretofore cited of Sir Isaac Newton and his dog perceiving the falling of an apple, the dog was seen as observing only the fact, while Sir Isaac Newton observed the law, which he called gravitation; yet not being developed in his divine consciousness, which perceives the absolute and divine, he could not tell the absolute cause of the phenomenon. The dog is in the manifestational sphere, while Sir Isaac Newton was developed in the manifestational and relational, but not yet in the absolute, but was capable of being developed in that sphere by induction. Man is therefore a microcosm. He has all those conditions which pertain to the universe. He is its fruit. There are three stages in the development of man: first, form; second, individuality; third, personality—to which Jesus made allusion in speaking of the development of fruit, saying that there was first the blade, next the ear, and after that the full corn. Man, standing at the head of the development, is the fruit of the universe. He is the grand ultimate of all preceding action. He is the footings-up of all that is and all that has been. There is no condition of being not a condition of relation in the wide universe which man does not contain in some department of his being; and just as he unfolds in his conscious nature, does he represent different spheres in the Spiritual world. If in self-lust, he registers his name in that department of the Spiritual universe called Gehenna, if in charity, he records his name in the sphere Paradise; and if in divine love—if the divine is so developed in him that it is a ruling love—he is registered in heaven; and then it is he perceives God. If he is developed like the Man of Nazareth, so that his Father's will is his will, so that he can bow submissively to it, whether it be to inflict pain and death or life and prosperity, he is born into the absolute or divine. This, then, is the simple law of unfolding. Man becomes in the Spirit-world what he is in himself. When you determine where his ruling love is, you have determined his sphere; and if he is to manifest to this world, he will manifest according to the sphere he is in. He advances by the same principle of induction as is concerned in the development of his personality. It is as the poet remarks:

"All angels form a chain which in God's burning throne begins,
And winds down to the lowest plane of earthly things."

Understand, then, each individual is a link in that chain, all put together in the various degrees of unfolding. So that "as each lifts his lower friends, can each into superior joys ascend." As you would raise yourselves, raise the man next below you. As you would labor to save yourself, labor to save your neighbor. Your salvation consists in saving others. There is no way in which a man so entirely defeats his own happiness as when he attempts to make that happiness his highest end. The pleasure-seekers will bear me witness that the real happiness is in performing some duty or fulfilling some end, not with a view to getting happiness. If a man seeks after right, he can not avoid happiness.

   Now you can understand that it depends upon you and me to determine our plane—to determine our condition in the Spirit-world.

Jesus said to his disciples that when he should go to his Father, they would see him no more, meaning that he should no longer appear in his form—no longer appear in the spheres of manifestation—Gehenna and Paradise. He can only be communed with by those in the same condition. But previous to going to his Father he told them, "A little while and ye shall see me." He was living then in his physical body, talking with his disciples through their natural understanding. He told them he was going to be gone a little while, and would return; but after that he would go to their Father, and they would see him no more. He first went to Paradise, from whence he could manifest himself. During forty days after his crucifixion he remained in Paradise, which joins the natural sphere, and manifested himself from time to time, endeavoring to open communication between the Spiritual and natural sphere. Having spent forty days developing his apostles as mediums, he went to his Father, into a sphere which is not one of manifestation, and they saw him no more. I do not mean that he went to a particular place, but that he went into a more interior condition; that is, he retired from the external to the absolute and divine, and of course could no longer be made manifest; and according to the description, he was separated from his disciples, and a cloud received him out of sight—not a literal cloud, but that interior condition of divine personality which made him invisible to them as a spiritual being, where he has continued from that time to the present. The second sphere, Paradise, is that in which angels are said to be God's messengers. God can not directly communicate his consciousness to us in this sphere. He simply give his consciousness to his angels, who translate it into the external sphere.

In speaking of the Divine Being as nearly as possible in external language, I would say that He is a personality, but not an individuality. Individuality is finite necessarily; therefore all the ideas originating from such an individuality are finite; hence if you attempt to portray the Infinite in your imagination, you make him finite, and just so sure as you attempt to make that finite image or idea represent the Infinite, that moment you involve yourself in inextricable confusion. You make an individual of God and make him finite. By personality, which is quite another thing, I refer to this principle of consciousness. That being only has attained personality where the subject arises and the object terminates within himself. That being is a personality alone who possesses self-existence and self-sufficiency. Now I standing before you am liable to influences outside of myself. An act arising from such influences is not strictly mine, not depending entirely upon me for its existence. If you influence me, and my act be a good one, you are entitled to part of the credit; if it be bad, you are chargeable with part of the censure. You can see that under this law of motive, which belongs to the first and second spheres of mind, no action depending upon outward condition is perfect, not being self-sufficient or self-existent. It belongs to the individuality; but when the act is of such a character that it can not receive outward influence arising from a sort of divine spontaneity, it is self-existent and self-sufficient, and the person capable of such an act may be said to be a personality; that is, he is becoming independent—attaining to a self-sufficiency and self-existence. An individual is neither. It is only that which receives. Hence man, who is said to be begotten the child of God, has another's self-sufficiency. All that he has he has received. Said Jesus, speaking from the natural plane, "I can of my own self do nothing. As I hear I judge. It is not I that doeth the work, but the Father that dwelleth in me that doeth the work." So you will understand what I mean when I say that man as a separate individual has a finite being, but in his connection with the Divine Being he becomes a personality, not of his own, but as a personality in God. The universal and eternal personality of God is in him. This is the relation we sustain as finite beings to the Infinite.

I expect not to convey my idea in a very clear manner. I can only point in the direction, and say investigate in that direction and you will find the infinite. I can only give a negative description of the infinite by saying what it is not, and ask you to pursue the positive in your inmost consciousness; and after a little while you will see some glimmering of the instinct infinite. Then all your doubts about the infinite will cease. You will then be able to perceive, although not able to describe, how it is that there is an infinite Father whose love and wisdom is over all his works.

CHAPTER VI.
MEDIUMSHIP.

My subject of discourse this evening is that of mediumship. There are two classes of mediumship, and only two: that which is external, that which reaches the consciousness through the region of thought; and the internal, that which reaches it directly in the affections. The most imperfect as a means of communication is what is known as the external, its imperfection being due to the fact of its having to employ in its communication certain signs or symbols, which signs or symbols each individual must translate by his own standard—by his own understanding. Its perfection as a means of communication depends, first, upon the perfection of the communicator; secondly, upon the perfection of the understanding of the individual to whom the communication is made. If the communication pertain to those things belonging to the common plane of the understanding, and the individual communicating and the one to whom the communication is made understand alike the symbols used, the method of communication is comparatively perfect. I am obliged to make use of certain natural words which are signs of ideas. If you understand these words precisely as I do, I will succeed in conveying my ideas. But if the slightest difference exist between us in the use of words, a perfect communication can not take place. You understand how this is. Nothing is more common in an audience like this than for different individuals to understand the speaker differently, though each individual heard the same words. But different conclusions are attained because each interprets by his own standard.

We can not be perfect in our external methods of communication any further than we each occupy the same plane in our communication, and understand alike the symbols used. If I were describing simple natural things, and describing them by natural qualities, there would be no difficulty, perhaps, in conveying a definite idea. I may not fail in describing objects by using such terms as "red, white, round, square, angular," because these terms are commonly well understood. So in regard to all the natural qualities of objects with which we are familiar. We have the correct elements out of which to construct a correct idea. Therefore, while I am communicating on the natural plane where we all possess the same consciousness, external language answers very well as a means of communication.

But suppose I attempt to go into a more interior truth—that which does not address each one's consciousness through the sense. I am obliged, however, to make use of external language; but as the interior truth is more interior than the natural plane, I must employ that language figuratively—must speak by parables, similes, and allegories. But the moment we begin to use language in that manner we are very liable to be misunderstood. The individual inclined to understand all things on the natural plane will very likely fail to get the spiritual idea which is figuratively conveyed. A truth expressed in figurative language, the figure being a natural one, will be understood by the one who takes it literally in one way, while he who takes it in a spiritual sense will get a different idea. So whenever we attempt to teach by parables, there is a very great liability of diversity of understandings. I refer to this to show that in communicating by external language, we are very liable to be misunderstood, unless we confine our subjects to the natural plane, and describe natural things by such properties as are common to all, and are accurate in putting them together, when we may succeed tolerably well. But if we omit any of these essential particulars, there will be almost as great a diversity of opinions as there are diversity of minds to hear the communications.

Many persons have thought that if they become mediums, and could see disembodied Spirits in the Spiritual world, and see how they are associated together there, they would become wise. As a mere observation of the vegetable kingdom serves simply to acquaint one with its various forms, but not with its uses, so a view of the Spiritual world might acquaint one with the fact that Spirits existed, of their employments, etc.; but the real interior truth, which is necessary to enter into you and make you wise, can not be acquired in this way.

The idea that we can get perfect communication externally, when we are imperfect ourselves, is altogether a fallacious idea. We depend upon our understandings for the meanings of communications addressed to us; and just so far as you are developed to understand perfectly, you may get a perfect impression. But just so far as it is above your comprehension, you are liable to misunderstand, and charge the fault upon your communicator. The proposition is simply this: You and I can not understand infallibly what is truth, unless we are infallible ourselves in the determination of truth. That which, of itself, is fallible and liable to err, can not determine the quality of infallibility; and whenever an individual affirms, upon some authority, the truth of any thing which, by his acknowledgment, lies beyond the plane of his intellectual development, he asserts something unphilosophical and false. That is only truth which, in our minds, corresponds to the actuality. It matters not who speaks, even though it be God; just so long as you must depend upon your understanding to interpret the meaning of what is said, you are liable to get a falsehood instead of truth. The question of truth depends as much upon you as the communicator. There has been a great deal of discussion about the infallibility of the Koran, of the Shasters, of the Vedas, of the Bible, and of the Book of Mormon. It has all proceeded upon an erroneous idea. Although the book may contain infallible truth, yet since you have to depend upon your understanding to interpret the language employed, you may fail to get the truth. You need to be infallible before you can affirm that you have the truth. You hand me the Bible, perhaps, saying that it is the Word of God, that it was given by inspiration of God, and that every word it contains is true, infallibly true. Very well. Do you wish me to receive the entire book of paper, ink, and calf-skin, to take the book and read it, and believe what it says? I must receive it as I understand it, and faith, therefore, corresponds to my understanding of the book. Is my faith in the book, or my understanding of the book? When a man affirms the infallibility of the Bible, he affirms the infallibility of his understanding. It appears that your faith can not be in the Bible, whatever it may teach. Your faith is only in your understanding of the Bible; and if your understanding happens to correspond exactly with the truth, you then have the truth. But if your understanding happens to be erroneous, your faith is in a falsehood. You affirm, then, that God teaches that which He does not teach; and you make your falsehood God's truth.

I want to make this plain, for here the law of outward communication is abundantly manifest. Look the world over and see how many different sects there are in Christendom: Baptists, Universalists, Presbyterians—I could not begin to name them all over to-night. They all take the same book and learn from the same source; and yet they come to very different conclusions. You may take any one doctrine which you may think the Bible teaches—and I will immediately find you a denomination who will deny it. One says that it teaches universal salvation, and another affirms that it teaches almost as universal damnation. Each man translates it by his own understanding; and each affirms that he has infallible truth. If they would just take this simple proposition, that that which is fallible can not determine the quality of infallibility—that upon these subjects the human mind is fallible, and therefore can not determine what is the absolute meaning of the communications—they would learn the source of all their errors. Men may be ever so honest, they will differ as a consequence of their constitutional differences. A man whose intellectual faculties are strongly developed, who will reason and demonstrate every thing rationally, will be a Presbyterian. Hence the expression "long-faced Presbyterian." It is very common for them to be long-faced. They are very actual, never have much feeling, and sit perfectly quiet. The minister must do all the talking, and the singers must do all the singing. The round, full-faced, emotional kind of man will not be a Presbyterian. You could not force him to be, because he judges by a different standard. He would be a Methodist. He would judge by the standard of feeling, and must have a great deal of noise; and a meeting is not worth a fig to him unless he can have a dozen round him shouting "Glory!" The Presbyterian, all reason, says God is omnipotent and omniscient; therefore He foreknew what should come to pass, and that, therefore, God foreordains whatever comes to pass. This is one of his cardinal doctrines. The Methodists says: "If that be true, man is not a free agent; but I feel that he is." He decides from feeling; the Presbyterian from thought. They can not read the same book and come to the same conclusion. There is a constitutional difference between the two. If they are to determine upon truth by outward communication they can not arrive at it. The man who feels pretty savage is ready to accept the doctrine of damnation. He feels that certain persons ought to be punished, and he thinks God will punish them. Here is another man who is all sympathy and love. He can not see how one man should, under any circumstances, want to injure another man, and he comes to the conclusion that all men are going to be saved. He thinks that if God is as good as he is, and he is sure He is, He will contrive some way to save all. That man will preach the doctrine of universal salvation.

So true is it, that phrenological differences point out different religious beliefs, that in almost any congregation you can sort out the Presbyterians from the Methodists, etc. This is a truth that God, nature, experience—every thing teaches. What is the use of quarreling about it, as long as we know that individuals hearing a discourse come to different conclusions. They do, they must, they will, and they can not help it. Until they come to a more interior plane they can never have one faith, one Lord, one baptism.

Now you understand what I mean by what is called the external communication. Suppose the Spirits make a communication, they make it in words. These words only address your consciousness through your understanding, and you make them mean according to your understanding of them. If the Spirit makes a communication by pantomime, it still appeals to your understanding, and depends upon your translation to give it significance. There may be error in the communication and in yourself, so that the error will be double. It is in this way that very many errors which have been charged upon the Spiritual world, after all, have their origin in the mistranslation and the misunderstanding of those who hear the communication. The teachings of Jesus, I think, are straightforward enough, if you will come to the plane of understanding to which they were addressed. Being spiritual, they can not be truly represented by natural ideas and language. For that reason he was obliged to teach by the use of parables, figures, and similes; and when he had done the best he could, the disciples, being educated in the natural plane, interpreted his language naturally, and, consequently, misapplied what he said. This is the fault to the present day. The truths he sought to communicate were peculiarly spiritual, and natural language could only represent them when used figuratively; hence he made choice of such similes or parables as would convey his meaning approximately, yet not without liability of material error. Hence he declared to his disciples, with whom he had been so long familiar, that they did not understand him, and could not, until the Spirit of truth should come to lead them into the truth of what he had taught. Language could not convey the truth, else it would undoubtedly have been so given. He knew how to describe the things of the Spiritual world so far as they could be described, for the Spirit had been poured out upon him without measure; but natural language could not portray the truths, scenery, and events of the Spirit-world.

The only perfect mode of communication is the interior method, or communication by inspiration. As a means of becoming wise, it becomes necessary for us to seek by some means to come into interior communion with the Spirit-world and Divine Being, since we can not by outward means arrive absolutely at the truth. If we will know that truth which is required to build us up into eternal life, we must ascertain what conditions are necessary to be observed to bring us into interior communion with the Spirit, so that without outward sign they can flow directly into our consciousness, and be written upon the thought or heart, as was said, "I will put my law into their understandings, and I will write it upon their affections." Thus truth must come to us without any recourse to Bibles or any other standard whatever. It so happens that the means by which we are to attain to interior communion are open to all. It is possible for every person to come into *rapport* with the interior spheres. According to one's ruling love or desire will be his affinity or communion with the spheres of the Spirit-world. If that be high, his communion will be high. If low, his communion will be low.

I will illustrate what I mean by interior communication. Suppose that some of you have a pain in the head. After your best attempts to describe it to me by natural language, I might not get of it a correct idea. But by putting myself in a negative condition to you, I could receive the pain myself, and be able to understand its character precisely. You thus communicate through the nervous medium interiorly. Many persons in public assemblies are liable to receive headaches of others by coming into *rapport* with them.

In each there is that which corresponds to all the media in the outward universe. There is a material earth, and I possess a material body. There is electricity, and I have electricity in my system. There is magnetism, and I have magnetism. There is a life-principle expanding all over the world, and I am in communication with that vital medium, and through it exert a vital influence upon others, and they upon me. This process of healing by mesmerizing is only coming into *rapport*, so that the vital forces of the healthy person enter in and strengthen the vital forces of the weak. Then there is a nerve-media existing around and in the individual, through which the pains of others are communicated to him. Pain in another causes an action in this nerve-medium which communicates the pain to me; just as my voice causes a vibration of the physical atmosphere, which action is communicated to your organs of hearing. The sounds I produce have certain meanings attached to them. If you understand them precisely as I do, you get a perfect communication. But any description in natural language of a pain would be inadequate. But when I receive it myself, I have in every respect an adequate idea of it. Very often, standing near individuals, I have told them what difficulties they were laboring under by experiencing them in myself. It is in this manner that clairvoyants frequently tell what ails their patient.

If I go on and describe your pains, there is nothing astonishing in it. I am simply in *rapport* with your nerve-medium. I am sometimes wondered at for this, but I might be a fool and yet do it. There is no wisdom involved in such a power; and it is erroneous to suppose, as some do, that because clairvoyants can tell them what ails them, they can tell them how to cure it. These powers belong to very different classes, but they may be united in the same individual, and he may be competent to discover disease and to prescribe its remedy. I refer to this simply to correct the false impression that clairvoyance is a wondrous power. It is one of the simplest powers in nature. It is one of the powers that may be made use of to bless; but if not properly understood, it may be made use of to curse. What is true in regard to this nervous medium is true also of thought. You often witness cases of this kind in mesmeric and magnetic experiments, when the subject and operator being brought into *rapport*, whatever one thinks the other thinks—what one wills the other wills. The idea is transmitted perfectly.

There is what is called thought-reading. This is governed by the same law precisely as that of which I have been speaking. One mind communicates its motion to the other by means of a medium, just as I communicate to your organs of hearing the vibrations of my organs of speech, through the medium of the atmosphere. When I have a thought which is an active condition of the mind, which may be denominated mental action, it is transmitted to the Spirit-medium or Spiritual atmosphere, and undulates through that until it strikes upon that receptive mind where the same motion is communicated, and the same thought produced, and the thought is impressed upon the consciousness. The one receiving it perceives it precisely as its communicator. Such a communication does not depend upon the Understanding simply for its perfection. This is what we call interior communication. According to the elevation of our Spiritual sphere in the sphere of truth or love, as we approach the infinite and absolute, will be the perfection of this method of communication. If we are very low, it corresponds very much to the external mode. But as we raise, it becomes more interior and refined, until finally, being unfolded to the plane of the absolute in our consciousness, perceptions, and affections, we shall come into direct *rapport* with the infinite, and receive communications directly from the Divine—not by any outward sign or symbol, but by the inflowing of the Divine thought and affection. This is the way and the only way that Spiritual truths can be communicated. The reason that Jesus of Nazareth did not communicate sufficient truth to the world to enlighten it, was simply because the world was not prepared to receive it. He said that he had many things to communicate, but they could not bear them. He also said that the man coming after him, living the life he had lived, should do greater things, because there would be a higher and wider plane. The world was too low, too animal, to receive his doctrine. For that reason he was obliged to go away, saying to his disciples that they did not understand him, and it was necessary that the Spirit of truth should come and illumine their understandings before they could understand him.

If I wish to understand Spiritual truth, no man or medium can be a medium for me, and I can not be a medium for you. Jesus of Nazareth can not be a medium for one of you, nor can God himself. Every individual who would understand the truths of the Spiritual world must be his or her own medium. God must write his law upon your understanding, and put it in your affections. If you want to become mediums for interior communications, you must become absolutely true in every thought, feeling, and affection—become absolutely pure in every desire and aspiration of your souls—become absolutely just in all your relations of life, so that morning, noon, and night you shall be inquiring and thirsting after righteousness. Such an individual will not need any outward signs to convey truth to him. But the person disposed to live in the outward world, to live in the enjoyment of his appetites and lustful affections, will require representations, if he ever believes in Spirits. He has to be addressed as a physical or sensuous being. If he ever believes in a future life, the Spirits have got to come and rap him over his head. These outward manifestations are designed to say to the sordid atheist, to the materialist, to the religious worldling, "You have a soul." It is for this reason that there is speaking with tongues, and that all the wonderful works are wrought in your midst. That is what makes Mr. Davenport's circles necessary for the vast majority of the citizens of New York. They are not sufficiently developed to understand Spiritual truth. These manifestations are necessary. They are not calculated to make you wise, but they can startle you, and prompt you to investigate; and they can give you such direction as will prepare you to enter into a higher and holier investigation of your relation to the world and to the Divine Father. It makes little difference whether they lie or tell the truth, provided they satisfy you that you have souls. If they were always to tell you the truth, you would be too dependent upon them. You have intellectual faculties—exercise them, and you will never find yourself in a position where you can not find all the light you need. A great many people who believe that Spirits do communicate, can hardly go to dinner without the consent of the Spirits. They make babes of themselves, and afterward become fools. If the Spirits tell me to do a thing which my judgment says I should not do, I tell them, "I won't. I will do the best I know how; and I would rather trust myself than you." I always get along a great deal better in this way than I would by getting Spirits to rap according to my expectations. They are not designed to become our governors. Sensible Spirits do not ask any such thing. There are ninnies in the Spiritual world as in this, who will be glad to become governors, if they can get dupes enough. The object of this external communication is to give outward evidence. The Corinthians had terrible times. Some people coming in said they were drunkards. Some said they were mad. Some spoke in tongues. Paul reproved them for this kind of talk. He told them that it was well to speak with tongues, but he would endeavor to make some use of it, and would rather speak five words with the understanding than ten thousand in tongues. The tongues are for a sign to those who are not believers. The man or woman that is not established in the faith that Spirits can communicate, needs these outward manifestations; but when established, it is all time thrown away to be chasing after these communications. Persons had better be in their closets, throwing their aspirations for a higher and holier life, and pray until, by their earnest aspirations, they call angels of the brightest spheres to come and be with them. They would find themselves getting along much better, and would give to Spiritualism a very different character from what it now bears in the wide world. I talk plain. I am in earnest. We have had nonsense and folly enough. It is time we become rational, learn the use of our faculties, and use them aright.

Everything has its true mission. Let, then, every thing be done decently and in order. If Spiritualism is that which is to redeem the world, we shall find it out by finding whether it makes us better; and if it will not make the world better, we want nothing more of it. We need no more raps than will save humanity. We need all we can get for that purpose. If Spiritualism takes that direction, it is a God-send to the world; and in whatever sphere the Spirit can work, let it work. I bid it God-speed. But I say to all, that if Spiritualism, in its faith and effects, does not tend to make you wiser, better, purer, and holier men and women, it is good for nothing. That Spiritualism which will not redeem you and me will not be sufficient to redeem the world. Therefore let our faith be shown by our works—be exhibited by the influence it shall exert upon our lives and characters in making us purer, better men and women—just men and women.

CHAPTER VII.
MEDIUMSHIP—SPIRITUAL HEALING.

When we make use of external language as a means of communication, our reception of truth does not depend so much upon who speaks, as upon ourselves; for it matters not who uses language, before it can awaken the idea in our minds, it must first be communicated to our understanding. Therefore though the communication may convey established truth, our understanding is quite liable to err as to the meaning of the communication. Though the communication were made by God himself, it might not convey the truth, because each man or woman would understand it according to his or her plane of development. The character of a communication is determined by the plane from which it is translated. The caution is, "Take heed how ye hear."

However credible and truthful an individual may be, he may be mistaken, and falsify in respect to facts and principles communicated; so that unless we have an absolute perception of the truth of that which is communicated, we can not affirm that we have the truth upon the subject in question. In holding communication with our neighbor, we find that A or B or C has always told the truth, and therefore when he tells us a particular event has taken place, we rely upon his word. Yet we know that he is liable to be mistaken, and to be under influences which may lead him to falsify, so that after all we can not know, upon the report of an individual, that a thing is true. It does not address that department of our being by which we are made as certain of it as we are that we exist. Hence we always make a difference between what we know and what we hear—between a report and our consciousness. One we say we *know* to be true, and the other we say we *believe* to be true. The difference is that between knowledge and belief. So if a Spirit should communicate to me ten thousand facts concerning my absent friends, every one of which I should find in every respect true on investigation; and if, again, that Spirit should come and communicate still other facts, I can not know that such other facts are true. The fact that that Spirit has before told the truth is not a positive proof that it will continue to do so. I can believe the statement to be true, but, nevertheless, my belief can not amount to positive knowledge. So that the questions often arise when Spirits communicate with external language, How are we to know that they tell the truth, How are we to know that they are the ones they purport to be? When a Spirit raps out on the table, or speaks or writes through a medium, that he is such a Spirit, and that such and such things are transpiring at some distant place, how are we to know that he tells the truth? We are not to know it, and can not know it. If we are to be accurately informed on that subject, that which is addressed to our understanding must come more interiorly into our consciousness than it can come through the ear, the eye, or the sense of feeling. It may be true; and give me time enough to investigate, and I can determine whether it be true or not. But if I am to act upon it without investigation, I can not know. I do not care if all the Spirits in Christendom testify to it, still I can not know; for that means of communication can not, in the nature of things, bring certainty—can not produce interior conviction in the mind.

I may be persuaded that a thing is so, and shape my course as though it were so; still I am liable to be mistaken. Therefore I affirm again, that this outward method of communication can not be relied upon for the communication of absolute or positive truth. You can not make it the basis of action as you can when you have clear and positive information; and even if it should become as reliable as the ordinary communications passing between man and man, still it will not bring sufficient certainty to make it the basis of action. I might give many other reasons why this external means of communication can not be relied upon as sufficient to give us the necessary information respecting our connection with the Spirit-world. It may give facts or tests which may prove to be sufficient to satisfy the mind of every inquirer that Spirits do exist and communicate. This is no unusual thing; but the point is to make them the instruments of communicating to us such information as from day to day we need, and upon which we must rely. Those who do thus rely upon their communications, and yield implicit confidence to them, nine times in ten show themselves to be complete dupes, and make themselves the laughing-stock of every sensible man and woman.

You will find in all parts of the country those who, if they can get a rap, say "Spirits, is it so?" and act according to the responses they receive.

Nothing can be further from the true use and design of these manifestations. My position is simply this: so far as these outward means of communication are concerned, they are designed for those who can not get a more interior view of their relations with the Spirit-world. If an individual is living in his exterior or sensuous nature, so that what comes to his understanding must come through his senses, then these outward manifestations are useful and necessary to satisfy him of the fact that Spiritual beings do exist, and have the means of communicating with us. But when he is fully satisfied on that point, he has received about all the benefit he can from these exterior communications.

There is another important point to which I wish to call your attention, and one which, if properly understood by those who investigate the Spiritual phenomena, will save them a great deal of embarrassment. It is this: that that class of Spirits who usually manifest themselves through public mediums, either by sounds, by moving physical objects, or by any other means before promiscuous objects, or by any other means before promiscuous public assemblies, can not generally be relied upon; and the reason is very obvious. It is well understood that an individual who is excessively sensitive to all moral influences—whose sensibilities are such that they can not endure the presence of that which is vulgar—are repelled by, or driven from, promiscuous circles or society; and, consequently, those who can endure the common influences of a public circle can not be of a very sensitive class. Take a medium who is exceedingly sensitive to external influences; who must be in just such a condition in order that the Spirits may communicate, and who requires that every mind in the circle shall be in a peculiar condition; and place that medium in a public circle, and you can get no manifestations at all, for the required conditions are foreclosed at once. This kind of mediums will not answer for the purposes of public circles; but if you get one that will answer for such purposes, that medium will be one who is excessively positive—one who can resist influences of ever so positive a character. As that medium is required to sit for all classes, as a matter of course he must be in a condition to respond to the kind of influences which are brought to bear upon him, or manifestations can not occur while such influences are present.

When communications are received through public mediums, the probabilities are that the communicator belongs to a very low plane of development, and that the communications can not be relied upon, whatever may be the professions of that communicator.

There is almost always an influence which belongs peculiarly to each public medium—an influence which seems to be a presiding Spirit, which that medium will usually recognize, answering to the name of "Jim" or "John." It is generally the case that this Spirit will be found on hand first, and is the one to do whatever is to be done; and he becomes the father, mother, brother, sister, or friend of everybody. I speak from experience on this subject. If this Spirit wants to be very accurate in telling you a name, he gets you to write down a list of names, and as your finger runs down the list, he raps when you come to the right one. If he knows the name, why does he not spell it out? This is a very reasonable question. Permit me to explain how these questions are often answered. In mesmerism there is at times a certain relation of the operator to the subject called *rapport*, in which condition the operator can transmit his mental motions to the subject. In case a Spirit comes into *rapport* with yourself, he answers all the questions you ask, even mental questions, and you come to the conclusion that you are really conversing with the one who purports to answer. If you ask whether you have a father, mother, brother, or sister in the Spirit-land, he will answer according to your perceptions; and the tests seem to be very good, though the Spirit is constantly answering directly from your own mind. This often occurs in public circles. Another individual, sitting next to you, who is very anxious to get equally good tests from his Spirit-friends, gets no correct answers unless he hands his written questions to one who has been found to be in *rapport* with the Spirit. I once knew an instance of this kind. A doctor came into a circle with about thirty mental questions, to which he desired to get responses; but he could get no answers, it seeming impossible for the Spirits to get the questions from his mind; but upon his writing them out, and handing them to a lady, who shortly before had succeeded in getting answers, they were all replied to without difficulty. The simple explanation of this fact is, that the lady was in *rapport* with the Spirit, and consequently her thoughts could be seen by the Spirit, while he could not perceive the thoughts of the physician, who was not in *rapport* with him. If you ask questions orally, it may be that the Spirit does not hear them, except through the medium's ears, so to speak. I might go on thus to great extent, showing the liability there is to be deceived in these public communications.

The circumstances of a public circle are exceedingly unfavorable to getting communications from Spirits of a high degree of refinement. The most that can be obtained under such conditions is some external evidence of Spiritual existence. The point to which I wish to call your attention is the almost universal fact that mediums devoted to external manifestations, while under the influence of this presiding Spirit, are under an influences to deceive, to cheat, which is almost irresistible. It does not matter particularly how good manifestations they get. I have seen this deceptive disposition manifested in mediums who could get very remarkable manifestations, such as the movement in the open light of a table with several men standing upon it. Not that they themselves wished to deceive, but they were almost irresistibly controlled by the influence surrounding them, and which must generally be present in a large circle. I have seen this many times when I knew the manifestations to be genuine. A skeptic, however, notwithstanding their genuineness, would, upon detecting the slightest thing like cheating, pronounce them all a humbug. There are but few mediums who could resist this influence which comes over them at times, inciting them to help the manifestations along a little, or to give them a little start, with the hope that they will thereafter get along without assistance. I refer to this to call attention to the influence to which mediums are at times subjected, not to condemn the mediums, nor to convey the impression that all these public manifestations are cheats. I have seen many which were not of this character. This cheating influence is attributable to the incongruous mental condition of a large circle, where no care is taken to secure harmony.

I offer these remarks as a caution not to get discouraged. You will meet with these things; and if the enemy can once catch you cheating, no matter how many good demonstrations you have given for months before, he has no hesitation in publishing to the world that it is all a cheat. He requires the medium to be very truthful, but he has no hesitation in lying himself. Being judged out of his own mouth, the enemy who takes advantage of the least deception on the part of the medium is as bad as the medium, and if he gets communications he must expect them to be marked by his character.

Permit me now to call your attention to the subject of healing mediumship. Man, as we have seen, possesses within himself the elements of all prior existence—in fact, of all existence, from dead matter to the self-living Jehovah. These elements exist in him in an individualized condition. He has composing his form individualized matter of various kinds, as electricity, magnetism, nerve-aura, which are connected with matter of a like character which is unindividualized. I need but say that all matter this side the Divine is of itself dead—that all life and consciousness flows directly and indirectly from the Divine Being, and that there can be no manifestation except as connected with the Divine Being. The idea that magnetism, electricity, or nerve-force has power of itself, is altogether false. They are only connecting parts in the universe, uniting the Divine on one hand with matter on the other. They are mere media of communication between the Fountain of all power on the one hand, and the recipient of power on the other. Let us for illustration observe a manufacturing establishment. One part of the machinery is perhaps concerned in scouring and cleansing wool; another part cards it into rolls; another part spins them into yarn; another part weaves the yarn into cloth; and another part dresses the cloth. Each of these parts seems to be disconnected from the other parts, and each seems to be accomplishing a specific end; but you will find that all parts are connected one with the other, and all connected with the primary power in the basement. In the water-wheel or steam-engine there is a power which puts them all in motion. The parts next to it are negative to it, and receptive of its power; and these parts, though negative to the principal power, are positive to those parts more remote. All parts are in motion, all moving as the primary wheel moves. Break the connection anywhere between the parts, and those parts beyond the connection cease to move. But establish the connection, and they will again commence their motion. Every part is negative to the primary power, but positive to all more remote from it than itself. No one of the parts has a power to move itself, and unless there is a connection maintained between the primary power and the several parts, they will cease to move. So with all media through which potential manifestations are made. Electricity has no power of itself. It is only by its connection with that which is nearer to the great self-existent Being that it derives all its power to act. Next comes magnetism, which derives all the power it possesses from the power which precedes it. Next is the life-force, which is negative to all nearer to God than itself, and receives its power from them, but is positive to all others. Next comes the nerve-force; and next the spirit, which derives all its power from the Divine Fountain. It is the medium through which all power is imparted to all that is more exterior than itself. I have the power to move my arm—by my will to make potential manifestations through this arm. If, however, by any means, you break any of the links out of the chain which unites the divine in me, through my spirit, with the matter of my arm—abstract the electricity, the magnetism, or nerve-force—I lose all power over my arm. Bisect the motor-nerve, which connects my arm with my brain, and my arm will hang lifeless by my side. There are all of the media there, but they are not continuously connected with my brain, and through that with the Divine Fountain. But if you will throw a current of electricity down the nerves of my arm, you will produce an extension of it. So you may withdraw the nerve-force, or the vital force from my arm, and it will cease to exist. My arm will be no longer subject to sensation, because you have broken the link between sensation and matter.

We then, as individuals, possessing in ourselves all these different media, which become receptive of influences, must come into connection with the Divine Fountain itself, if we would receive power from it; for we can impart nothing which we do not receive.

As spiritual beings we become receptive of this influence through our spiritual nature, but impart it through our lower nature. To become a medium of potential action or manifestation, I must have the power to impart to that medium through which the power is to be manifested. To affect you nervously to relieve you from pain, I must be able to impart through my nervous system that power which I received through my spiritual nature. To be able to operate psychologically, I must receive through my interior being and impart through my outward being—must first have the powers of receptivity, and, secondly, must possess the powers of impartability. It becomes just as necessary to have a good, healthful physical development to be able to impart, as to have a good spiritual development to receive the power. The individual becomes stronger as a medium in proportion to his development in receptivity and impartability.

That Jesus was so much more powerful than others was owing to the perfectly harmonic development of his different natures. Our power to exert healing influences depends upon our development. The higher we are developed—the nearer we come to the great absolute Fountain of all power—the more largely will we be receptive of that power.

Jesus being fully developed in his religious and spiritual being, was in conscious communion with the Father and with Spirits of the most exalted character, and received largely of the Divine power. He was always aware whether he had the necessary power to perform any work. Being so fully unfolded as to perceive the causes of the disease to be cured, he knew beforehand whether it was worth while to make the experiment. He knew what was to be done to bring the individual into a condition to receive that which he needed to restore him. Therefore, when called upon to perform a cure, if the individual was not in the right condition, he commenced to bring him into it, requiring them to come into a certain condition called faith or belief. That he might perform the desired work, he required the assistance of those around him. When he went to Nazareth, where he had been brought up, and where he was looked upon as an ordinary man, his right to teach was called in question, and his learning doubted. What was his success there? Mark says he did not succeed, because of their unbelief. He could not command the conditions which were necessary to impart his power, and he could do no mighty work there, except to lay his hands on a few sick folks. Another writer referring to it, says, "He did not many mighty works there, because of unbelief." We all know that Jesus said, "A prophet is not without honor save in his own country." He had to keep away from Nazareth simply because the state of mind was such that he could not control the conditions necessary to produce his mighty works.

Within three weeks before his crucifixion, when going to Jerusalem to attend one of the feasts, his brethren called upon him and said, "If you do these things, show yourself openly, for no man doeth these things in secret, and yet seeketh to be known openly; for," says John, "his brethren did not believe on him." Christ, even with his high degree of receptivity, found it necessary at times to call to his aid surrounding minds; and he could not always perform his work without faith being reposed in him. The question was very often asked by him, "Believe ye that I am able to do this?" When he had performed the cure, he immediately said "It is faith that did it." They had no faith in him as the Son of God, as supposed by some, but simply in his power to work a cure.

I desire to enforce the idea, that if we wish to be mediums of high and exalted powers for the removal of diseases, it becomes necessary that we should be highly developed, not only physically, but spiritually and religiously. A high order of the absolute religious development is very essential to great power as a healing medium, because this highest nature, this absolute nature, in man, much more than any other, serves to unite him with the absolute Fountain of all power. The highest development of this religious nature in man is necessary to give him a clear perception of the nature of disease and the means for its removal. The man who has this religious faculty highly developed, needs not that any man should say anything to him of man, for he knows what is within him. Clairvoyant mediums know very well that that condition which enables them to see most clearly the state of the individual is that which is high and exalted; for when their thoughts and aspirations seem to be ascending—like the odor from the flower—there is a sort of conscious exhalation going forth permeating every thing around the individual, and he sees and feels clearly the condition of everything by which he is surrounded.

There is nothing in the world which summons the human being to such a degree of activity as that which we call the religious nature—there is nothing which takes hold of him so deeply. What other influence in the world could cause a mother to destroy her babe, but the stimulating influence of this religious nature, coming up as it does from the deepest fountain of the soul? Make a man believe that his religious nature requires sacrifice, and he will make that sacrifice, cost what it may, simply because his religious nature wells up so strong when it is moved, that there is nothing outward which can resist it. When the individual's religious nature is highly developed, it is more powerful than all his other natures.

We will become healing mediums just in proportion as we are developed in this religious nature, so that we shall become more receptive and perceptive, and be enabled to exercise stronger mental power to accomplish our results. But a healthy physical development is quite as essential to good mediumship as is a high and healthy spiritual development. Good organs of impartability are required. Secure a good harmonic physical with a good harmonic spiritual development, knowing that you are receptive on the Spiritual side, and impartive on the physical side.

There is much folly connected with mediumship. That such should be the case with people so profoundly ignorant as the majority of mankind are with reference even to their having souls, is by no means surprising. Many people suppose that if their hands are touched, a Spirit has got hold of them, and is about to make something great of them, and they set themselves up as something wonderful. If they can perceive any influence coming upon them, it is attributed to a Spiritual agency. It may be so and it may not, because there are other than Spiritual agencies. I once witnessed the curing in five minutes of an individual who had been blind for three years. This, told to the world as an instance of Spiritual healing, would appear marvelous; and if I had happened to do it on the platform, before the people of New York, they would have thought I had almost performed a miracle. It is probable that not a particle of Spiritual influence was exerted in the case. The individual performing the cure did not suppose that he was a medium, though some would not hesitate to publish it to the world as a remarkable instance of healing by Spiritual aid. The blindness was doubtless caused by a paralysis of the optic nerve, and required only a little action to restore the sight. The individual proceeded according to the usual modes of mesmerism. The cure was not half as difficult as it would be to get a sliver from under the nail, nor was it half as mysterious.

A case of the restoration of hearing, by placing the fingers in the ears and taking them out suddenly, is also within my knowledge. Such cases are frequently circulated as evidence that Spirits do cure. The cure in this case was doubtless effected by a strong mesmeric current passing from the fingers of the operator over the nerve of the ear. As honest men and women, we should be careful about publishing these things as instances of Spirit-healing. We have abundant *genuine* evidence of what Spirits do. Attributing to Spirits that which is not produced by them, tends to make us dishonest with ourselves and our neighbors. Were due caution exercised in this matter, we should not need *half* the evidence which is now required to convince the world that Spirits do exist and communicate. When it is observed that everything is attributed to Spirits, the world will not believe us even when we tell them facts.

I know that Spirits *do* communicate—*do exist*. It is not with me a matter of conjecture at all—I KNOW it; but there is no occasion to make persons believe that every thing comes from Spirits. I ask Spiritualists to be more careful, more dignified in their investigations in these matters, and they will find that there are facts enough before the world to convince it of the truths of Spiritualism, when you can convince the world that you are duly cautious and not easily misled. I do not wish to lie for Spirits, nor do I wish them to lie for me.

CHAPTER VIII.
CONDITION OF THE SPIRIT IN THE SPIRIT-WORLD.

In order that I may present the general condition of the Spirit in the Spirit-world in the most intelligible form, it will be necessary for us to enter into a very close and accurate analysis of what constitutes the Spirit, because if we do not well understand what constitutes the Spirit, we shall only be able to conjecture of its condition of happiness in the Spirit-world; and if we are to have a close and rigid analysis of the Spirit, we, can only have it by having a close and rigid analysis of our own conscious being, because we can know nothing but our own consciousness; and if we are to learn of the condition of Spirits in the other world, that condition must be translated into our consciousness, and we must find it therein recorded, or we can only conjecture of their condition.

Then the first point to which I wish to call your attention, is that which distinguishes the condition of absolute consciousness from that condition which goes to make up individuality—that which is universal and applicable to all, and that which is only individual and applicable to each and every individual. Every individual has the means of determining how much of this being—"I, myself"—belongs to the external and finite, and how much to the internal and infinite; because that which makes me to differ from you is finite; but that which makes myself or yourself one and the same with every other individual being in the universe, is infinite. Therefore the first point of investigation is to ascertain what it is that makes you and me differ from every other individual being in the universe—in what that difference consists—because when I speak of you as a Spiritual being, I speak of you in view of that difference, and not in view of that sameness.

You understand that individuality makes the difference between us. My individuality makes me to differ as an individual being from you. The question now arises, what constitutes my individuality, this "I, myself"—

what enables me, when speaking of the events Of childhood, to say, "When I was a child," though every thing has changed that pertained to my individuality as a child—thoughts, feelings, tastes, pleasures, form? What is it that connects the events of twenty or thirty years ago with my present being?

I wish each one to go down into his own mind and solve that problem, because if we are to talk about Spirits we must learn about ourselves. When each man understands thoroughly the Spirit that is at present speaking to him, he will be able to form some correct ideas respecting its condition in the Spiritual world.

Upon examination, each will find that there is within himself a principle of absolute consciousness—a principle which is self-conscious, which represents itself to itself, and is not represented by any thing but itself. It can not be analyzed. It is absolute in itself. To prove to you that your consciousness of identity has undergone no change, I need but attempt to prove to you that you are the same individual that you were when a child, by referring to scars made upon your fingers in childhood, which still remain, by calling to mind traits of your childish character. All these proofs you would consider very much inferior to that proof afforded by an affirmation within you, which rises above all outward evidence. It is that to which the Book alludes when it says, "As he could swear by no greater, therefore he swore by himself." Although in your physical, intellectual, and moral being you have changed in every thing pertaining to your finite consciousness, yet there is that within you which tells you you are the same. Let one change follow another to eternity, you will not lose your consciousness of identity.

That which makes you differ from others does not enter into this absolute consciousness of identity. In other words, the thought, feeling, and affection which characterized you at any particular time of life has nothing to do with this absolute identification of self. Nothing by which the world knows me, or by which it knows you, enters in to form our inmost identity. We have an identity which lies deeper than everything external; and it is this identity, which admits of no change, which says that we are the same, and will forever remain the same identical beings to all eternity. No change of position, no change of character, no destruction of reputation, no conversion of happiness into suffering, presents the least difficulty in the way of identification. The man who has fallen, been ruined in reputation, and is steeped in suffering, finds no difficulty in identifying himself as the same being who was once good, respected, and happy. He does not say that there was once a being who was happy and good, but who has changed and become another being, but he says that the character and position of this individual identity has changed, while his identity has undergone no change. I wish to call your attention to that principle of absolute consciousness in you, by means of which you know yourself, but by which nobody else knows you. You know that that principle in you does not constitute your individuality. It constitutes your personality; but that in you which is undergoing change, and develops from a lower to a higher degree of knowledge, constitutes your individuality. This unchanging, ever-present, conscious identity is the very divine life within you, from which you derive all life. This outside identity, which thinks and wills, is no part of my immortal nature, separate from this divine principle within me. This outside consciousness can never be in any other state than the finite. For wherever you have succession and duration, you have time. Where you have succession in extent, you have space. In regard to this outward finite nature, one change follows another; and if change follows change, there must, in respect to such change, always be succession; and where you get succession, you must necessarily have time. Hence the spirit, in its finite nature, must always be in time till it shall cease to change; when progress ends, time will cease with the finite. This is a proposition so plain that no mind can for a moment be lost in considering it.

We can form some definite idea of the Spirit-world by first learning something of ourselves. You know that this conscious principle within me and you knows nothing about time or space. Suppose I instantly become unconscious, and remain so twenty-four hours, and am then suddenly restored to my consciousness. During this twenty-four hours there has been no additional record of events made within me; therefore that twenty-four hours is obliterated so far as my consciousness is concerned. I take up the time where I left it. To the unconscious there is no time. To the unchangeable there can be no time. Time is but the marking of succession. The inmost principle by means of which we become acquainted with ourselves, knows nothing about time. When one is restored from unconsciousness to consciousness, he knows instantly who he is, but he can not say how much time elapsed to the outward world. Clairvoyants who pass into a condition of unconsciousness to all exterior things, have no recollection of what occurs while they are in that condition, though they may have been in it for several hours.

I knew an individual once to be put into the mesmeric condition, who was unconscious in his normal condition of what occurred in the mesmeric state, though he was in it for five hours, and during that time performed many interesting experiments. At the time of sitting down to be mesmerized he was in so great hurry that he thought he could spend but a very few minutes' time. On being brought to consciousness, he started off again in great haste, supposing that he had sufficient time to attend to his business, showing clearly that he had not been in a condition to mark succession of events.

The inmost principle of consciousness which identifies me of to-day with what I was thirty years ago, does not, of itself, notice time, except as it is connected with this outward part of me. It counts time by changes; but when you come into itself and separate it from those changes, it does not know time at all. Between my infancy and the present time it has been a constant now. It is the presence of the infinite and eternal in man, and the means by which he is connected with the infinite and eternal. It is by the presence of this infinite and eternal consciousness that man knows that he possesses a finite and changeable nature. It is a lamp within, which shines out and reveals to him his finite consciousness, and the changes transpiring there. So man has two selfhoods, an inward, and an outward which is changing from day to day.

When I speak of you as an individual being who differs from me, I speak of your outward, changing selfhood. But when I speak of you in your inmost consciousness, I speak of you in your inmost selfhood, in which you do not differ from me.

It is by this inmost consciousness that I know that I am. It reveals myself to myself by just the same law by which you are revealed to yourself. There are two methods of addressing the outward selfhood—from without, and from the infinite within. Where the individual consciousness is addressed from within, the communication is made to the affections, whence it flows into the understanding. When it is addressed from without, it is by representations of that which addresses it. But when I go to the Spiritual world, I go with this divine consciousness, this constant, unchanging consciousness within, but not as a principle which belongs to me, which is individualized within me. It is just as universal as God. It is the divine consciousness which is unindividualized within me, and wherever that is, I must be, because of the ubiquity of this divine principle. If there were any point from which this could be excluded, and into which the individual could be thrust, he would be annihilated.

What we need is to bring the external consciousness into unceasing relation with this internal consciousness. That which does not come into such relation with this absolute consciousness does not become a part of our finite selfhood—a part of our immortal selfhood. Standing before you I perceive your countenances, because your images are brought into a certain relation to this absolute consciousness within me. Now when they come into unceasing relation to this unchanging consciousness, they become a part of my external, finite selfhood. Memory is the result of bringing events into such relation with this consciousness.

Looking at man, then, as possessing an absolute consciousness which never changes, and an external consciousness which is constantly changing, and which alone causes one man to differ from his fellow, it is apparent that if individuality is preserved upon entering the Spiritual world, each must take with him so much as causes him to differ from others. Whenever this external nature would represent itself to another, not having a consciousness of its own separate from the divine consciousness, it comes under the law of exterior communication and representation. Therefore it is never present in the mind by itself, but by that which represents it there. If we would learn how it is that a Spirit represents itself in different places at the same time, we must learn the law of representation. I see my audience, by which I mean I see that which represents you to my consciousness. You are presented to my consciousness by means of a medium which comes between you and me; and according to the accuracy of my faculties to perceive, and according to the accuracy of this medium to represent you to my consciousness, will be the accuracy of your representation in my mind.

I see you now by the medium of light; and you all see me at the same time. I am here and only here, but you all see me in your various positions. You see me by means of the light which takes my image into every part of the room. Though actually present in but one place in this room, yet by that which represents me I am omnipresent in this room. The great law of representation is that we perceive a thing, not by itself, but by that which represents it in our consciousness. Hence according to the ubiquity of the medium will be the ubiquity of the representation. In this room the medium light is ubiquitous, and my image is just as omnipresent as the medium. The same is true of every other medium by which presence is represented.

I, as a finite spirit, am conscious only by means of the divine consciousness within me, which imparts and reflects consciousness to my outward nature. My outward consciousness is like the light of the moon, which is the reflected light of the sun. The real consciousness within me is that from which I derive my external consciousness. Whenever I, as a spirit in my external consciousness, would represent myself to you, I must come into some medium of representation—some medium which will be to my spirit what the light is to my body. The medium of light will not represent me, but there is a medium which will. This, the Spirit-medium, is vastly more refined and ubiquitous than light. Standing here as a spiritual form, and giving off spiritual undulations, just as my body reflects the undulations of light, wherever the Spirit-medium extends, there my image will extend. And whenever an individual comes into *rapport* with this spiritual medium and sustains a certain relation to me, he will be able to perceive my presence, because I am brought to his view by that which represents me.

Many suppose that a person whose mind is separated from the sensuous influences of the body, or brought into the clairvoyant condition, can go to a distant place, as to London, and see an individual to whom his attention is directed. He tells me what the individual in London is thinking and saying, yet hears what is said to him here. If the individual in London were to be thrown into the clairvoyant condition, and have his attention directed to the clairvoyant here, the two could readily converse together. Space is not noticed by them, though it might be by carefully going over the space and observing a succession of objects. Being brought into *rapport* with each other, each can observe the thoughts and feelings of the other. This is done by virtue of a simple law; and there is no mystery in it. The medium which unites my organs of speech with your organs of hearing, extends through the entire room, and my voice is as ubiquitous as the medium which communicates it. So in regard to this Spirit-medium, which is the medium of communication between the clairvoyants. By that medium, London, Canton, or any other part of the earth, is present here. Persons who mistakenly suppose that persons in the clairvoyant condition leave their bodies and make journeys to distant places, get up many curious theories to account for the body and spirit being held together. Their error arises from a mistaken conception of the actual condition of a Spirit. You see readily that a Spirit can be addressed externally only by that which represents that which addresses it. Apply to the case in hand the same law by which you see and hear me, and substitute for the media of light and atmosphere the Spirit-medium, and you will have no difficulty in understanding how it is that Spirits can be represented in different places.

Persons sometimes meet with difficulty in explaining the apparent fact, that person in the form are sometimes seen as though they were out of it. I recollect several cases where persons were said to have been seen and conversed with at places very remote from each other; and it was supposed that the spirits left their bodies and went to these distant places and represented themselves. It is very easy to understand how my spirit can appear in real Spirit-form and speak to one a hundred miles away from here. It is done by what is called psychologic representation. If I come into *rapport* with any mind yet in the body, which mind is in *rapport* with me, I can create any spiritual image in your mind that I may see fit to make; that is, I can cause the image in me to reproduce itself in you—so that that image in my mind shall be reproduced in your consciousness, as the object before the camera daguerreotypes its image on the prepared plates. Now suppose that between us one or more guardian Spirits are passing. The Spirit coming into *rapport* with me, and having a full and perfect perception of you, can, by the intensity of his mental action, daguerreotype my image upon your consciousness. You then perceive me by the psychological action which that Spirit exerts upon your mind. It is in this way that we can apparently meet and see each the other's form, just as though it were present. But if we were more susceptible, there would be no necessity of having the intervention of a guardian Spirit. If we are both so developed as to clairvoyantly perceive one another, the conversation can go on, though both are in the body, and you in London and I in New York. We see each other as though we were present one with the other. It does not follow, however, that my spirit is present in two places at the same time; but that which represents it is universally present. The question may arise, why we can not, upon passing into the clairvoyant condition, see all the Spirits in the universe—because they are all in *rapport* with this spiritual atmosphere. I will explain. Suppose we have ten thousand strings strung from the ceiling to the floor, and they are made to give forth certain sounds. Now all that have the same degree of tension will give forth the same sound. The vibration of one will cause all the others to vibrate which have the same degree of tension. Take any stringed musical instrument, and vibrate one of the strings. If any other of the strings has the same point of tension, it will vibrate. Now when my spirit comes in contact with the Spiritual sphere and sustains the same relation to any Spirit that the strings sustain to each other, I can see that Spirit. Upon the same principle I may see all who are in the condition to respond to my spirit. When my consciousness will undulate to their conscious vibrations, I perceive them, and not till then.

If a Spirit is not present, except by that which represents it, it will appear useless to open doors to permit Spirits to enter, for a door is as transparent to the medium by which they are represented, as a pane of glass is to the medium of light. Jesus appeared in the midst of his disciples, though they were shut up; and when the time came for his disappearance, he ceased to be seen, not by going out of the door or window, but by disturbing the conditions by which he was represented to their consciousness.

In respect of Spirit-mansions, etc., in the Spiritual world, we are very liable to mistake representation for actuality. We are very liable to mistake images of things—creations, so to speak, proceeding from the minds of the Spirits—for actualities. We are very apt to perceive animals. Some think that animals have a living form and exist in the Spiritual world; but I pretend to say that it is not true. I know very well how they appear there. I know very well how it is that persons suppose they do exist, and why Spirits in the Spiritual world appear to have their dogs, cats—their pet animals. To them they are actualities. Nevertheless, I understand that the idea that a cat or dog has an immortal soul is not only inconsistent with any principle of philosophy in the universe, but is contradicted by every principle of philosophy. To say that a cat or dog is immortal is to affirm that to be immortal which God himself can not make so. The condition of immortality can not pertain to the mere animal being. The representations of animals, forests, fields, and things of this kind, have no basis upon that which has a material or actual existence in the universe. They are only developed under the law of representation. Man has a sort of creative faculty, by which he forms the images which are mistaken in the Spiritual world for actualities. When Spirits are thinking of animals they have seen in this world, they throw out their images, and the individual who chances to be in *rapport* with these Spirits sees these images, and thinks they are actualities.

If you will only investigate the law of representation, you will have no difficulty in accounting for these things in the Spiritual world. Man makes these—they are not real. God makes all that is real in the universe. Man works in the sphere of representation, but God works in the sphere of actuality.

Had I time, to-night, I should be happy to go into a careful investigation to justify the conclusion that dogs and cats, etc., are not immortal. There is no end to be subserved in their being immortal. If the animal were to go to the Spiritual world, there being nothing to address his consciousness, he would virtually have no being. Whenever a mind goes where its consciousness is not addressed, it ceases to be mind. If there is any place in the universe where consciousness ceases to be addressed, there consciousness must cease to be. What would there be in the Spiritual world to address the consciousness of the animal who has been developed only to the perception of physical objects?

Again, between the nerve principle (the highest principle developed in the animal) and the absolute or divine principle, there intervenes the Spiritual principle, which, being developed in man, makes him receptive of the highest or divine consciousness, and makes him immortal. The animal lacking this principle can not be immortal. According to aspirations the animal puts forth, according to its mental phenomena, according to every principle, the animal is not immortal. Nevertheless he has a representation in the Spiritual world, according to the law of representation.

Every individual who is conscious of an existence as an individual, has that within him which constitutes him an individual; and as he goes into the Spiritual world, he takes with him that individuality. This individuality in its inmost joins upon the absolute, through which it perceives its own consciousness, and by this connection is unfolded in the facts, truths, and principles of the universe.

CHAPTER IX.
ORGANIZATION—INDIVIDUALIZATION.

The experience of man has been such, in respect to organization, that all prudent and careful men and women are beginning to have fears for the welfare of a cause when it assumes the shape of an organization; and they have just ground for fear; for the experience of the past has been such as to justify them in supposing that evils arise out of organizations. Their tendency usually has been to beget a party feeling, or that which corresponds in the organization to selfishness in the individual. It is natural that every individual should love himself better than others, and when individuals associate together, they acquire a spirit of individuality—a selfishness which pertains to their particular society or organization. Individuals who unite in religious organizations entertain a sort of selfishness in reference to their particular denomination. The Presbyterian, for instance, likes Presbyterians a great deal better than Methodists, and the Methodists likes Methodists a great deal better than Presbyterians, and prefers to bestow his favors upon Methodists. In fine, the general tendency of this kind of organization is to lay in men and women the foundation of a selfishness in addition to their natural or individual selfishness.

There are many reasons for the evil results of organization; and if we continue to organize upon the principles observed in organizations of times past, we may expect that the same evils will continue. I propose to inquire whether there is not a natural basis, and endeavor to discover the causes of evils for the past, so that we may know how to rectify them and guard against them in future.

Every operation in nature tends to individualism. From the moment you begin to watch matter, every process is found tending to individualization. The elements which now compose our bodies originally existed in a general unindividualized state or condition. The material elements of our bodies, and the media through which the material elements were controlled, in bringing them to their present position, existed originally in an unindividualized condition; and when each particle was brought under a certain process that it might receive vital affinities, it was with reference to the formation of an individualism. Nature labors constantly to organize and individualize, and you and I owe our individual existence to this tendency in nature; and the same law operates in society. The fact that there have been so many organizations, shows that there is a natural tendency to organize. The great difficulty attending all organizations has been the departure from the law of nature—the law of affinity or attraction—for Nature works by the law of affinity, never by the law of repulsion or excretion. The law of excretion is only applicable to those elements which are to be rejected. External force has never been applied by Nature to aid her. She does not bring external force to hold the elements of the tree or rock together, nor to hold together the organs of the animal.

Individualization is the result of an inward power which attracts one part to cohere with its fellow. Nature is very careful to observe the law of affinity; and the moment you bring any element which should not enter an organism, repulsion immediately operates to prevent its entrance.

Hate is at times defined to be a less degree of love, and love sometimes is very negative. Repulsion is also defined to be a less degree of attraction. A stone thrown into the air is drawn to the earth by the power of gravitation. But the balloon which is subject to the same law, instead of coming toward the earth's center, rises. It does not rise because the earth does not attract it, but because the atmosphere, for which the earth has a greater affinity than for the balloon, causes the balloon to recede and make room for it. The case of the balloon illustrates the law of excretion. The position which each particle is to assume in the system is determined by the vital affinities imparted to it in the stomach. If any particle loses its vital affinities, it occupies the position needed by some other particle; and the new particle accordingly displaces the old. But I wish to impress upon the mind the fact, that Nature's law of individualizing is that of affinity, and that Nature does not apply external force to build up her individuals. However, before any particle can be taken into an organization by the law of affinity, it must receive a peculiar impress or affinity, and an affinity suited to the particular organization into which it is to enter. It receives that affinity by passing through a natural process. If it enter without a vital affinity, it will enter in as a stranger, as a disturber of harmony; and the tendency of the organism will be to reject and throw it off. What we here learn from Nature, we may apply to organizations, religious or otherwise. Each of us is a particle in society. But before we can be organized harmoniously, so that each shall be found in his specific place, each must be prepared for that organism by receiving the vital or spiritual affinity which is necessary for that organism. You can not make A, B, and C into a community unless they have the true impulse, any more than you could go into the field and gather clay, sand, etc., and mold them together, and make a man or animal body. You can not hold men together in an organization by outward restraint, and have them fulfill the office of a genuine organization, suited to the development of the spirit. The method by which society seeks to organize itself is like the method by which God created our first parents. Each individual should be fitted to become a member of an organization by being placed where he will receive the appropriate vital affinity, and leave the affection of his nature to point out his true position, whether that of head, hand, or feet. The great difficulty in all past organizations is that the natural law has not been observed. Organizations have usually been formed with reference to exerting force, either moral or physical. They have organized by that which is external rather than internal.

The first requisite for an organization is a nucleus of the character of the organization you wish, which nucleus may consist of one, two, or half dozen individuals. The individual who is seeking to establish an organization must look for the nucleus in himself, not in his neighbor. The idea of looking out of yourself for an organization is all false. The idea that you must look to a distance for some being out of yourselves as a representation or reflection of the perfect attributes of Deity, is erroneous. The individual who feels the need of an organization must first understand that that organization must be built up by the law of affinity; and that as each individual becomes a particle to be incorporated into the organism in his love and affection, he must grow to retain his position. The vital principle must be felt by himself. If he wishes to redeem the world, he must commence by redeeming himself. If he wishes help in redeeming the world from its various evils, he must first find in himself that spirit which he wishes infused into the helping association.

If a principle has not succeeded in saving me, I need not hope that it will save the world. Therefore, when we are about to organize a society upon any principle, the first thing to be ascertained is whether this principle has saved us. If not, we may just as well drop it. If a person wishes to form an organization to make the world Christian in faith and practice, you should ask him if he has been made a Christian in faith and practice. If he wants fidelity to truth and righteousness, ask him if he is faithful to truth and righteousness. Let the individual be tried by that which he wishes to accomplish. If he can not stand the test, he is not the proper person for a nucleus for such an organization. Before one mourns over the lusts of the world, let him look after his own lusts. So in respect to every thing necessary to make a truly upright man, a man who shall live in all good conscience before God and the world, and before the inmost of his own soul. Let him see to it that after he has made a perfect examination of his own breast, there is nothing found lacking. Let him be so satisfied with his examination of his own character, that he will be content to have mankind redeemed up to the plane he occupies. Then let his life be the incarnation of the principle. Let the world, when they look upon him, be constrained to say, "He has been with Jesus," if Jesus is to be the model of the church. Let his life correspond exactly to the high and beautiful ideal of the church he is wishing to have established; and then an influence will go out from him which will become attractive to all who, like him, are thirsting for that life. He will find it unnecessary to throw out catechisms, because there will be the true affinity which will come forth from the character, and attract all who, like him, are hungering and thirsting after righteousness. Form a church by the application of external tests, and there will be conflict all the time; while concord will characterize one formed in accordance with the natural principle of organization.

Spiritualists have become very numerous. I doubt whether there is any other class of believers so numerous as those now known as Spiritualists. They now number millions, and they are men and women who have come from under the restraints of authority—of external law—a "thus saith the Lord"—and have assumed the prerogative of acting for themselves. One article of their creed has attached to them the name of "Spiritualists". They profess to believe that our disembodied Spirit-friends are near to us, and hold converse with us; and when any one says that he believes in that, he is called a Spiritualist. That appears to be the only test. But that external belief or assent is not better as the basis of an organization than is the creed, "I believe that God fore-ordained whatever comes to pass." The idea that such an assent could be made the basis of an external organization is entirely unnatural and supremely ridiculous. If you should attempt to organize upon such a basis, you would be guilty of the error into which all previous organizations have fallen.

Many entertain the idea, that because we have overcome our blind deference to authority, refused to be ruled by the "thus-saith-the-Lord"—because we have come to the conclusion to examine all questions for ourselves—we have taken all the steps necessary for our own reformation and that of the world. But what has been the influence exerted by this new faith—New Philosophy as it is sometimes called—upon the lives and character of those who have accepted it. You say, perhaps, that when you drive all the church dogmas out of the way, there will be nothing in the way of redeeming man. So far as you are concerned, they are driven out of the way, and what has been done for you? How much better are you morally, religiously, than the man you call a bigot? You wish all the world to be converted to a belief in the possibility and actuality of Spiritual intercourse; but suppose that all the world are converted to this faith, what are they to gain if it produces no better fruits in them than in you? While we are trying to get the motes from our religious brother's eye, is it not possible that we have very extensive beams in our own? We are calling for organization to unite the moral power and energy of the millions of Spiritualists; but if the influence of Spiritualism has not served to redeem us, how are we to expect that it is to redeem the world? If *Spiritualism* does not save *you*, how are you to reproach the church for its inconsistency in sending its missionaries to convert the heathen to what they themselves do not practice—when even slave-holders are received to the bosom of the church, while the slave toils in the rice and cotton swamps of the South, while the babe is torn from its mother's breast. If the church were to turn round and point out similar inconsistencies among Spiritualists, what would the Spiritualists of New York reply?

Spiritualists should see to it that the work which is wrought in them by Spiritualism testifies what will be its work in others. If it does not touch their own character; if it does not make the false man true, the corrupt man better, what reason shall we give in favor of its being received by the world? We have Spiritualists enough to convert the world if they were only *spiritualized*. There is the difficulty. It is one thing to be a *Spiritualist*, and another thing to be *spiritualized*. What we want is something that shall take our Spiritualists and spiritualize them. We want to find some key which shall open up a fountain deeper in any man's soul than has yet been opened by these manifestations—which shall call out higher, holier, and purer aspirations after eternal life than have yet been called out. We all know this. We find every thing on the right hand and the left to admonish us that when the whole world shall have been converted to our faith, it will be a bad world still. What then is needed is, that you and I set about a work which is peculiarly intrusted to us. We shall then redeem the world.

I must look for the coming of my Lord in my own affection. He must come in the clouds of my spiritual heavens, or he can not come for any benefit to me. I must place myself in that condition that shall invite him to come and reveal to me the way by which I am to be redeemed; and then I shall learn the way by which you and all mankind must be redeemed. When all my falsehood, injustice, selfishness, lust, appetite, and passion are dead, and when the God of heaven shall live and work in me, then there will be laid in my soul the foundation of that true spiritual affinity which shall go forth, not seeking others to unite with me, but, of its own plentitude, uniting with me those who have the same affinity—uniting us stronger than any creed. We shall not then be obliged to ask permission to join or withdraw from such a church as we should establish, but each man would join or withdraw according to affinity or repulsion. Each man will stand upon his own responsibility. I shall not be responsible for you, nor you for me. I stand not here to give you Christian character, nor you to give me Christian character. Each man must have a communication for himself with the Fountain of all love and truth. We must all draw our water from the same well, and it will become in us a fountain springing up into eternal life.

Each must prepare himself for the kind of church he needs. Let each seek to redeem himself. The Spiritualists of New York and throughout the United States will be ready to form a church just as soon as they have prepared themselves to give forth the true affinity; and you will find that it will not be necessary to have any creed or catechism, any thing external by which to try the faith of this or any other movement. If you make up your mind to lead a true life, to speak the truth, to be pure and just—if you make up your mind that whoever comes within your influence shall breathe in of your truth and righteousness—you will find none will seek to come unto you unless they desire to breathe that atmosphere.

The difficulty of the old organizations has been, that no man or woman supposed it was necessary to make themselves the representatives of that which they believe to be necessary for the redemption of the world. Their faith was not in their own righteousness, but in the righteousness to be wrought in somebody else. They worked to be righteous by proxy. They hoped to be saved by the righteousness of another. Consequently they organized upon an external basis, as their organizations were not based upon a true affinity of character. They did not understand that they must possess the true character, consequently they did not labor to attain it. The individual seeking to form a church only labored to form a creed. He did not suppose it necessary to form a character which he wished to have infused into the church. The world, however, can never be saved until the false opinion that it can be saved by the righteousness of another is done away. The world would put away its lusts, appetites, and passions, were it not that it loves them. Although they do not confer the happiness the soul feels it needs, they confer more happiness than they know how to obtain from any other source. Therefore the world is not willing to put away its lusts, appetites, and passions, and to become absolutely pure and just; and if you will offer them a religion which offers to save them from the consequences of sin, and yet permits them to continue in their sins, they will willingly pay for it, especially if its ceremonies and the decorations of the church gratify the taste. If they can have nice things in their churches, it is considered nearly as good as to put them in their parlors. But tell them these things will avail them nothing, that they must love their neighbors as themselves, that they must put away lust, appetite, and passion, and you offer them a salvation they are unwilling to accept.

CHAPTER X.
WHAT CONSTITUTES THE SPIRIT.

The idea which has sometimes prevailed, that when the spirit enters the Spirit-world it becomes divested of certain states of affection, certain loves or delights, and that it becomes so changed in its character or station as to seek its delight in some other direction, is very general among Spiritualists. They believe that all our evil passions and affections pertain to this body, and that when the spirit leaves it, his disposition to do evil or to enjoy the fruits of his evil desires ceases. Now, I wish to investigate this subject thoroughly upon principles which commend themselves to every individual's consciousness.

That which constitutes me a conscious being does not differ from that which constitutes you conscious beings. So far as the element of consciousness itself is concerned—so far as it enters into the mind—it is the same in every individual. Your individuality or mine does not consist in the fact that we are conscious, and possess in ourselves a consciousness, but it consists in that of which we are conscious. That which causes me to differ from you is that which comes into a certain relation to that consciousness.

This conscious principle within the spirit, whether in the body or out of it, is the Divine principle. It is to this spirit what the sun is to the natural universe. It is the light and the heat of the Divine sun shining within the individual, revealing him to himself; so that if we become familiar with this first proposition, so that we understand one another, our deductions will flow naturally, and we can understand perfectly whether we are on the side of truth or not. Understand, then, that it is not the fact that you possess a consciousness within you, which causes you to differ from me and every other being. We are all alike in that respect. But when that consciousness begins to shine out into your individuality, and look after your thoughts and affections which have arisen out of your individual development, and which have grown out of individual relations peculiar to yourself, then this conscious light and conscious heat, this conscious understanding and affection within you, begins to reveal to you your individual selfhood—that which constitutes you an individual being separate from all other individual beings. That which pertains to my character pertains to my character as an individual being.

This individual affection which distinguishes me from you belongs to my exterior or outer consciousness. So then, when I speak of character, I speak not of this inmost principle which has never changed, and never can change, but will live on unchanged, because self-existent and self-sufficient —not of the God within—the Divine breath living in the soul—but of that which is exterior of that which derives its life, understanding, and perception from the light which this absolute consciousness throws out. That which pertains to my character enters into my individual and finite selfhood; and it is by what is found there that I am to judge myself, and the world is to judge me. If you were to come to my inmost character, you would then come at the absolute and infinite which exists in me and in every other individual, without which man could not be a conscious being at all. Separate man from this conscious consciousness, and he would cease to exist. It is by the harmonizing of his finite perception with the infinite perception that he lives in God and God in him. All there is of life, of conscious being, is but a reflection of this absolute consciousness; just as the light of the moon is but the reflection of the light of the sun. Extinguish your sun, and your moon could give you no light. Separate man from this absolute consciousness, and he would have no finite consciousness. Then that which constitutes you and me conscious beings here and hereafter is not this absolute conscious principle within, but that which comes into unceasing relation to it, by which we are made conscious of that which is.

I have thought, feeling, and affection, which pertain to me as a finite physical being; and I am made aware of that thought, that feeling, and that affection by the presence of this absolute principle within me; but at the same time they do not take their character from this absolute consciousness. Hence we hear persons talk about forming characters. But character is to be considered in a double sense. All possess this inmost character, and hence it is said that every individual in his inmost is divine. But that Divinity, that God within him by which he lives, and without which he could not live, constitutes no part of his individual selfhood. It is the Jehovah in the soul, by which he is revealed to himself. That character in man, I grant, never changes.

It is the external individual character to which I wish to call attention in a special manner. Now that character which makes me an individual being, and by which I become wise or foolish, good or bad, true or false, is constantly undergoing changes, and is developed under laws growing out of relations which I sustain to material and spiritual things and influences which operate upon me from both the natural and spiritual plane. This finite character is the one by which I am to be judged.

I wish to examine man in his relations to the present and the future, and ascertain, if possible, how much of this finite character will continue with him after he enters the Spirit-world, because upon this point there is a great diversity of opinion. It is really one of the vital points of Spiritualism. How, then, is this external individual character unfolded? It depends upon the ruling love in the individual, as well as upon his intelligence or perception. We know that the individual dwelling in selfish lust unfolds his selfish character by doing that which he thinks will furnish him self-gratification, and we determine his character by the character of the impulse which governs him. The individual who has known no higher impulse than this desire for self-gratification, finds it impossible to conceive that a person can act from a higher impulse; but one who has experienced in himself a higher and purer impulse than that which looks after self-gratification, can easily understand how it is that men and women can act from higher impulses; but still he may not be able to understand how they can act from an incorruptible Divine love—love in its infinity, in its spontaneity, going forth of its own Divine fullness, and bestowing blessings upon all who come within its sphere.

If we look out into society, we see individuals living down in the lower departments of their nature. We wish to reform them and mankind, and talk about Spiritualism doing wonderful things for the world, by way of breaking off the chains of superstition which have bound people down in ignorance; we talk about its removing that superstitious bigotry which causes one man to persecute another for not thinking as he does. We expect it is going to diffuse a liberalizing influence, and thus *re*form the world. What do you mean when you speak of Spiritualism reforming the world? You mean that it is going to change the characters of those living in it. You thus virtually affirm that this external character that pertains to you, and me, and all others, is the subject of change. We understand, then, that your hope for the reformation of the world is based upon the expectation that the individual character shall be changed. And how are you to change that character? You hope to change the character of the unfortunate female, and place her upon a higher and purer platform, by changing her ruling love, correcting her false opinions and false understandings—by having a purer affection to govern her, and a higher understanding to direct her. You hope to cause her to walk more in harmony with her highest destiny. To persuade the inebriate to give up his cups, you desire to create in him a love and respect for the welfare of mankind—to implant in him a ruling influence which shall elevate his character.

When you look at yourselves even, you see that your character is undergoing a change. When a boy, there were certain kinds of amusements in which I took delight. Moral and religious exercises were nothing compared with my hoop, top, etc.; but when I became a man, and began to be manly in my aspirations, my character had changed. So it has been with us all. That within us which we call character, we suppose must be forever subject to change. Each of us as we progress, hopes to change, to become wiser, better, purer. He who boasts that he has never changed his opinion, virtually says that he has not progressed. He who claims that he feels as he did twenty years ago, boasts of his own shame. Our hope to progress implies our expectation of change from that which is false to that which is more true—implies a change of this external changing principle within us, which constitutes our individual character—our finite selfhood.

The question arises whether we shall take this distinguishing character with us into the Spiritual world. We need not be left to conjecture here, if we will only enter into a philosophical examination of what will constitute our character. You see clearly, that what constitutes you an individual being here, is that which is external to the absolute consciousness within, and that when you lose this, you lose your individuality—that if it should be absorbed, your individuality would be gone, and you would be taken up by the principle of general absorption, and would cease to be as an individual being. But when you understand that that which constitutes you a spiritual selfhood pertains to your thoughts, your understandings, and affections, and that nothing outside of your understanding enters into that selfhood, in which you live, and by which you know yourself, you will perceive that if you do not take that with you to the Spiritual world, you will take nothing with you that is yours. If you leave that behind you, or so change it as to make it represent another and not yourself, as a matter of course, when you go to the Spiritual world, *you do not* go there.

The idea has obtained to a considerable extent, that this material body is the cause of our lusts, passions, and appetites, and that these will die with it. It is my opinion, however, that the body, so far as the matter itself is concerned, does no more to degrade us or injure us in any wise, morally, than does the matter composing any other material substance. It has only become an instrument receptive of certain conditions, as the horse-shoe magnet has become receptive of certain magnetic conditions. We talk about the attraction of the magnet as though the attraction were in the iron. But the attraction is between the positive and negative conditions, which are present in the iron; and when your bring the different parts of the iron together, you bring the conditions which they contain into proximity, between which the attraction exists. So it is with this material body; it is made receptive of conditions. The matter entering into this body needs to go through a certain process, after it is taken from the rock, before it is fit to enter into the human system, because the matter which enters into the mineral kingdom undergoes a certain change by which it is fitted for the vegetable structure; and is then brought into a certain relation by another principle by which it becomes receptive of another condition, which other condition is essential to it if it would enter into or become receptive of the essential condition. So that the particle of matter passing through the vegetable kingdom passes through it for the purpose of being made receptive of a higher condition; and when it passes into the animal it has come into relation to another power, called the nerve-power, with which it was not in relation when in the vegetable kingdom. It is brought under the influence of this nerve-power, and made receptive of another principle. And thus one particle of matter, in passing from the mineral up to the animal kingdom, goes through that elaborating process, simply because by being brought into relation with certain media it becomes receptive of certain higher conditions of which it was not before receptive. The conditions do not change the character of the matter at all. They pertain rather to the spiritual than the material department of this being; so that when my body is brought to a certain condition of development, it becomes receptive by a sort of induction of new conditions. Certain relations are established between my body and spirit. My body depends upon certain things for nourishment, and my spirit depends upon my body for certain assistance. These relations make my body subject to a law of consciousness; but that law of consciousness does not pertain to my body. My body is but the instrument by which that consciousness is acted upon from the external world. When I experience pain in my finger from placing it in the fire, it is not my finger that smarts, but there is a consciousness in my mind which experiences the pain, from the report of nerves which come to the surface in my finger. Separate these nerves, and I may hold my hand in the fire without feeling the least pain; yet if the finger were pained, it should feel as much after the nerves were separated as before. Though the sensation appears to be at that point, it is after all in the mind. The body is but an instrument by which sensations of a peculiar character reach the mind. Those who have had arms amputated, have experienced pain seemingly in the fingers at times in consequence of the exposure and irritation of the nerves which go to the hand. It is sometimes conjectured that they have spiritual fingers, but it is not so. There are instances of persons experiencing pain seemingly in the toes, after the leg has been amputated. This is in consequence of the exposure and irritation of the nerves which go to the foot. Furthermore, the individual who has been mesmerized—who has had his mind separated from the sensuous influences of his body—may have his body dissected to pieces without experiencing any pain, notwithstanding the least injury done to the person who is in *rapport* with him will be instantaneously felt, as though the sensation were in himself. He can not be reached through his nerve-system, but you can reach him through the nerve-system of the operator, whose mental condition is impressed upon him. The sensation, however, is in his mind, not in his body, notwithstanding he locates it as though it were in his body. Numerous other proofs might be adduced to prove that though the body is the means through which the mind is reached, yet the sensation is all in the mind. Man makes use of his body for the gratification of all his sensuous desires; all of which originate in the mind. I do not deny, however, that a sense of lack, not pain and disease, may be induced in the body by certain courses of action—by disturbing the nervous system. But that is a thing entirely of itself. But there are other influences originating in the mind, leading the individual to seek gratification in horse-racing, gaming, sexual indulgences, etc. In ten thousand instances the stimulating influences to various acts arise in the mind, and form a part of the mind. In the majority of instances the body is simply made the instrument for the gratification of lustful desires. Did the usual habits of thought permit, it might be demonstrated, in various ways, that lustful desires originate in the impure condition of the spirit.

There are certain impulses pertaining to the body *in its relation* to the body. An instance of such is the sensation of hunger. I do not mean to say that the body has the sensation of hunger, but that it is awakened in the spirit by a demand which the body makes upon the spirit for material to supply its need. There are the sensations of thirst, heat and cold—diverse sensations of this kind which come to the spirit through the body. But that impulse which leads the individual to seek gratification at the horse-race, the brothel, etc., has its spiritual original, and flows out of the depraved condition of the spirit; and the body is not responsible for it, though the body may be destroyed by such impulse.

When we enter the Spiritual world, if we recognize ourselves at all, we must recognize ourselves by that which the absolute consciousness reveals to us. I do not recognize myself by the principle of absolute consciousness within me, but by that which it reveals to me. When I go to the Spirit-world, I must take that with me of which I must be conscious, else I shall not take my individuality with me—else I become annihilated. Just to the extent I leave my affections behind me, shall I be annihilated as a spiritual being. When I go to the Spiritual world, I must take my character with me—that which is made an integral part of my spiritual character by its development in me. Of course, then, wherever I go that must go. The love which rules within me must go with me until that ruling love is changed, or until some holier love shall call me to a higher plane of action. I am prepared to maintain that when we go to the Spiritual world, we shall take with us all the love, affections, thoughts, feelings, and sentiments which characterize us as individual beings. Every thing which causes me to differ from you here will cause me to differ from you when we enter the Spiritual world. I will retain my spiritual selfhood by the same laws by which we maintain our selfhood here. I believe the testimony of all Spirits who have spoken to us concerning it, is that the difference between the sensations here and there is so slight that it is difficult to tell when one has entered the Spiritual world. Many times have Spirits testified that they had to make many examinations after entering the Spiritual world, to satisfy themselves that they had left the body. That is, their sensations, thoughts, feelings, loves, and affections underwent so slight a change, they did not recognize any change in passing to the Spiritual sphere.

If that individual Spirit changes his character there, it must evidently be by some law operating upon character. We know perfectly well that if you were to bring an individual into New York who has been given to a certain kind of pleasure, unless he can find the same channel of pleasure here, he would feel miserable. Let any one of you get in the habit of going night after night to the theater, and you will by-and-by acquire such a habit that you will be perfectly wretched unless you can go there. You make resolutions to break up the habit; but often break your resolutions, and will feel miserable until some other love takes the place of your love for theatrical amusements. The poor drunkard often, in the midst of his dissipation, resolves to put away his cup; but when again he comes in the presence of the bottles and decanters, his mouth begins to feel thus and so, and he can not help drinking. The habit is so fixed upon him that he can not break it up, unless something can implant a stronger love within him.

As is our condition in this world, so is our state in the Spiritual world. How often does an individual feel that there would be no source of enjoyment for him in the Spiritual world if he could not find certain pleasures there. The beef-eater will continue to have a desire for beef, unless some other gratification can come in to supply its place. So it is in reference to every means of gratification. Upon the same law that the good desire the good and true, would the individual who has been a pleasure-seeker in this life seek in the Spiritual world for his accustomed gratification.

In the Spiritual world the Spirits have the means of gratifying their desires. Beef-eaters have the means of gratifying their desires. Not that they have any Spiritual beef. They have a mode of getting beef there different from ours—namely, by representing it and growing it on their own plantations. Spirits also enter into their former pleasures by coming into *rapport* with those here who have tastes like their own. If all their passions and lusts are to be dropped, how are those to know themselves in the Spiritual world who, during a whole life here, have been dead to every feeling and sentiment? Will they know themselves by their truth and justice? They never had any. How are they to know themselves, except by that for which they were known here? It is evident that they must carry their animal impulses with them. Gratification for these impulses are procured by the law of mental sympathy—the Spirits getting into *rapport* with those on the earth who have desires similar to their own, and taking thus the gratifications in which they delighted while in the body. It is for this reason that so many dark, benighted Spirits are found revealing themselves to the world. I am aware that, in these latter days, the idea has been advanced that Spirits, when they leave this body, get rid of all this filth. The truth is, the body was the cleanest part of them here. The idea that when a Spirit leaves the body he gets rid of all his impurity, has caused many to greatly venerate Spiritual communications, and attach to them much authority. I remember that it was with much deference that I listened to the first communications which came from the Spirit-world; but I very soon learned that a Spirit was not necessarily wiser because of his separation from the body, and that he required quite as much watching as one in the body. Not that they are below the world; for when you have taken an average of the justice and wisdom of the world, you will find that the standard it could set up would not be very high. When you look over the earth and witness the very low state of character of the human race here, why should you wonder that Spirits of a very low character should hover around us and manifest themselves to the world.

There was some philosophy in Dr. Beecher's conclusion, that the manifestations were Spiritual, but devilish; for the majority of these manifestations come from the very lowest Spirits. There is no use in denying it. But the fault is all our own if a Spirit of an undeveloped character comes in communication with us and controls us; for I have power, which is superior to all their finite power, to prevent their controlling me. If I will live the life I should, I can be protected from all such influences. If a Spirit of a low character comes into *rapport* with you to control you, it is your fault. It is because you are not in that true condition of soul by which you come into *rapport* with Spirits of a pure and wise character. It is nevertheless unphilosophical for any individual to say that, because there are low Spirits, he will have nothing to do with Spiritual communications. It would be equally unphilosophical to say, because there are good Spirits, that all Spiritual communications should be received.

In respect of developing mediums, I wish to say, that if they are to be developed for curiosity's sake, they had better remain undeveloped. But if it is desired to bring them into conditions to redeem them, it is all very well. But no person should permit himself to become passive in his feelings and affections while waiting for Spirits to come and develop him as a medium; for in that condition he will be liable to be influenced by bad Spirits. He may become the instrument of one of the lowest and most debasing influences, and may be influenced to commit the most filthy and disgusting deeds. While the body should be passive, the affections should be ardent, the soul must send forth its most earnest aspirations.

You need not read from the Bible or the Koran. What is needed is to keep your hearts right. Let the aid for which you seek have strict reference to keeping the affections right. We need to guard against being influenced by those low Spirits who are waiting round us to seek self-gratification. If you wish to commune with Spirits, you yourself must determine what shall be the class of Spirits with whom you will commune. If you would commune with Jesus, you must come upon his plane. If you would commune with the Divine Father, you must become like him. You must assume the character of the class of Spirits with which you wish to commune. By observing this law we need not have so much of this low manifestation. We need a higher class of communications to convince the world. The objections to Spiritualism is not that there are not enough facts, but that their character is such that the world is not willing to accept them.

CHAPTER XI.
LUST.

"Every man is tempted when he is drawn away of his own lusts."—James *Letter*, chap. i. 14.

Lust may be defined to be the desire for self-gratification. The forbidden fruit is that which seems to be desired to make one happy, and is sought after, not for the purpose of supplying a need, but to gratify a desire.

Man's constitution is such that there are needs pertaining to every part thereof; and those needs are indicated by awakening desires; and when the need is supplied, a pleasure or gratification is experienced, which is a sort of plaudit of "Well done;" and all legitimate pleasure or happiness which man is constitutionally fitted to enjoy arises from complying with the proper demands of his being. All constitutional demands of the being man have strict reference to constitutional needs; and the life and energy making that demand will not be disregarded. It will not suffer the being to find rest until the demand is complied with. It will create restlessness and disquiet; and the individual will give expression to that life and energy in some direction, if he does not in the true one.

Man possesses within him immortal energies, or he could not be immortal. He has that which is essentially being and life, and which can not be destroyed. Hence his divine energies will act with omnipotent power to him, and he will be constrained to submit.

Here, then, is to be found the fundamental distinction between true and false impulse—true and false action. That impulse which arises within, indicating a need of some department of our being, is true and legitimate; and all proper action which tends to supply that demand, without conflicting with any other need, is true action. All other action and impulse are illegitimate. The distinction between the two classes of impulse and action is easily made, by an appeal to our own consciousness. By a careful examination, we can tell at once whether the impulse to perform any act for

ourselves arises from a sense of need or from a desire of self-gratification; and whether the impulse to perform any act for others arises from a near or remote prospect of self-gain, or from a sense of fitness, justice, or goodness of the act, in forgetfulness of separate self.

In the very outset I postulate the following as undeniable truth: All *true* desire in man has respect to a need of some department of his being, which, when truly supplied, will harmoniously develop him in respect to every other department of *his* being, and also in respect to all other beings necessarily connected with him. That all *true* happiness or enjoyment which he is capable of possessing must flow as a consequence of truly supplying these needs; and that while every need of his being is fully supplied, he will be in the enjoyment of all the happiness he is capable of desiring, and consequently will not desire happiness on its own account.

I postulate further; that until every need is supplied, man will feel a sense of lack, a desire for something which he does not possess, the tendency of which will be to stimulate him to activity in some direction; and unless his activity is directed to the proper supplying of the need, it will be misdirected, and will tend to *deprave* rather than to *improve* his being.

Hence I postulate further, that when man feels within himself a desire for happiness, he has demonstrable evidence that these are needs of his being which have not been supplied; and any attempt to fulfill his desire, short of finding out and supplying the true need, will be derogatory to his highest good and destiny, and will consequently fail of conferring that which he seeks, happiness.

I therefore postulate further, that happiness or enjoyment is not to be sought; that if it come at all, it must come unsought; that it is a necessary and inseparable incident of the true life, by which is meant that life which in its activity fulfills its every need. That happiness which is sought after is never found, simply because it is not an *end*, but only an *incident* of being; and that while man is absorbed in the pursuit of pleasure, he must necessarily be unmindful of his needs, and thereby he will neglect their demands.

Here we have the foundation laid for examining the distinction between the true impulse, known as love in the various planes of unfolding, and that which is to be characterized as lust. The true impulse is that which indicates a need of some department of our being, and which prompts to activity, looking to the supply of that need, independent of any gratification which it may promise. The false impulse is that which prompts to activity, not in respect to any specific need, but in respect to the gratification which it may afford. This latter impulse is known as lust.

For the purpose of distinction I shall denominate the true impulse, *love*, as being a manifestation of the Divine Father's wisdom and goodness, in whatever plane it may be found; and I shall denominate the false impulse, *lust*, as being a manifestation of that which tends to lead to selfishness and antagonism, and makes the interests of finite self overrule those of infinite self, or the selfhood of the divine.

In the scale of being there is every plane of unfolding, from the unconscious to the divine consciousness; that is, there is every sphere of divine action and manifestation, from the monad to the highest angel, and consequently there are many degrees of love as the true impulse to action. It has its sphere in the plane of physical need, in the plane of intellectual and moral need, and in the plane of religious need; and it is exalted just in proportion as it approaches the absolute or divine.

As there is a true impulse belonging to every plane of unfolding, begetting the proper enjoyment in the conscious plane when its demand is properly complied with, so also is there every degree of lustful desire seeking gratification in every plane, differing in grossness according to the *means* by which it seeks its gratification.

Reflection will satisfy every truth-seeking mind that desire for self-gratification, as an impulse to action, has its basis in self; and, from its nature, makes itself the center of attraction, and becomes a sort of an absorbent, seeking self-appropriation; and whenever it makes an expenditure, it is with respect to that which is to return. And it never gives without the hope of receiving in return a full equivalent.

This principle of action is from its nature finite and antagonistic, upon the principle that that which it seeks to appropriate to its own benefit and make its own, can not at the same time be appropriated by another; and hence the desire of self-appropriation naturally leads the individual into antagonism with others.

This finite and selfish impulse is the very opposite of the infinity and unselfishness of the divine. Its imperfect and antagonistic rule of action can not harmonize with the perfection and harmonic action of the divine. As the finite in every respect is the negative and opposite of the infinite, so this finite impulse in the individual is in every respect the negative and opposite of the divine impulse. It is for this cause that there is such an antagonism between the principle of love and the principle of lust; an antagonism which must continue until the divine shall bring all into subjection—until the finite shall, in its principle of action, harmonize in the infinite, or until God shall become *all* in *all*.

Having already postulated that all true and legitimate desire in the individual has strict reference to the needs of the individual, independent of any promised gratification, and that the gratification incident to the supply of such needs was the measure of all true finite happiness, I now proceed to illustrate this truth by an appeal to the experience of all who hear me.

Happiness, in its general sense, is the fulfillment of desire. And the more complete is the fulfillment of every desire, the more complete is the happiness; and happiness can not be perfect until every desire is fulfilled. If in fulfilling the desire of one department of our being we neglect the needs and consequent demands of another, we may obtain temporary gratification, but it does not answer the full demand of our being so as to confer happiness. On the contrary, while we gratify a lust, we resist a true demand, and purchase gratification by disease and suffering.

The individual, ignorant or unmindful of the true demands of his being, and intent upon self-gratification, must forever fail of obtaining happiness, because in his lustful pursuit he does not heed the real demands of his entire being, and therefore he does not minister to their needs; and hence can not obtain ease and satisfaction. All pleasure-seekers can testify as they have testified, that their pleasures are more in anticipation than participation. Their happiness is in the future, and seldom if ever in the present. The time never comes when they find every desire gratified, and consequently they are never quite contented, therefore never quite happy. The very desire after happiness is that which defeats it. The finite belongs to the present; the *past* is his schoolmaster, teaching him in the *present* how to receive the future. His duties and needs are of *to-day*, and those which pertain to the morrow will come on the morrow, not before. "Sufficient unto the day are the evils thereof," and sufficient unto the day are the *duties* and *pleasures* thereof. Man can not take being and existence by anticipation, neither can he take their true incidents in that way. All anticipations of pleasure by which the individual is made to live in the future, to the neglect of the present, are lustful and illegitimate, and antagonize with man's true nature and destiny, and consequently tend to defeat true happiness. That this is so, all human experience affirms. That this must be so, the philosophy of true happiness demonstrates.

There is no room for controversy upon this point. It is most evident that true happiness can only flow to the finite by fulfilling the true desires of the finite, and that complete satisfaction can only take place when every true desire or demand is complied with.

Now it must follow that every true desire is indicative of a real need of the being in which it exists; and consequently when every need is supplied, every true desire must be gratified, and true happiness must be the result. And as every need has respect to that which pertains to the *present*, every true desire belongs to the present, and asks present fulfillment.

From considerations of this kind it becomes evident that anticipated pleasures are illegitimate, and belong to the school of lusts, and do not tend to beget true happiness; and that just in proportion as the individual is absorbed in the anticipated pleasures or duties of the morrow, he is disregarding the true law of his being, neglecting present needs, and laying the foundation for defeating the very end he seeks. Man, as a physical, intellectual, moral, and religious being, has needs pertaining to each and every department thereof, and consequently in supplying these needs he becomes receptive of pleasure from every department of his being. When he is truly and harmoniously unfolded, all his needs are orderly and harmoniously set forth; and when he truly complies with their demand, his delights or gratifications blend or flow together in one harmonious stream, and his whole soul is filled with the divinest melody, instinct with the *present* God. But note, the moment he neglects a single need, or misdirects the energies of his being, there is not only a strain which is not represented in the choral anthem of God, but it is caused to vibrate discordantly with those strains which are represented, and instead of a soul pulsating with the divinest melody and joy, you have it harshly jarring to the discordant notes of antagonism and death.

The principles of this philosophy affirm that man must attend to the needs of every department of his being, if he would develop harmoniously. The Divine, in the plenitude of his wisdom, has given to man nothing superfluous. His physical body, with its needs, is just as essential to the perfect man as is his spiritual being; and its demands are as imperative in their sphere. And man is as really obeying the Divine in truly administering to his physical as to his spiritual needs; and the pleasures attending the true administration are as true and just in their sphere as are those pertaining to more exalted spheres of being and action. He who despises and afflicts his body to benefit his soul mistakes the divine order and method, and in afflicting his body wars with the true interests and destiny of his immortal being. The disposition to afflict the body for the benefit of the soul is that higher manifestation of the selfish and lustful principle turning its weapons purposely upon itself. Its aim is self-gain, and, through that, self-gratification. Hence the cloistered nun, the solitary monk, and the stern ascetic, of whatever school, are violating the divine method and law as much as is the pleasure-seeking worldling. They are as really under the dominion of their lusts for self-gratification as any other class. Their expenditure of worldly pleasure has respect to the spiritual, which they hope thereby to obtain; and, like any other selfish being, they only act with respect to some expected gain, bringing with it enjoyment or gratification.

The great error of the world is that it does not distinguish between the true and false impulse, giving rise to true and false action, out of which grows true and false development, bringing existence into antagonism and false relation.

Said the Divine Teacher, speaking of little children, "Of such is the kingdom of heaven." The infant at birth instinctively obeys the law of its being, and it continues to do so in every department of its being which does not come under the rule of its conscious, voluntary action. When it feels the demand for food to nourish and develop its infantile body, it indicates that demand by its restlessness and complainings; and when the demand is supplied, its complainings cease. It does not ask for gratification beyond the supply of its needs; *that* it does ask for, and must have to give it quiet. During this early period it eats to live, and continues to do so until, by its development, another nature with its needs is brought into conscious existence, and neglected. Then the unsatisfied demands of that other nature impart disquiet to the being, and he begins to search after gratification. It is in this way that lust is begotten. It is never felt until the demand of some need is neglected, and it is an immutable law that such neglect must beget lust; and hence whoever feels the demand for gratification of any sort hears the voice of God within proclaiming a neglected demand, a perishing need. He sees the cherubim of God standing at the gate of Paradise, with a drawn sword of flame turning in every direction, guarding the tree of life. Thus man's lusts proclaim his imperishable needs, and, when truly understood, they are but the echo of God's voice calling upon him to return and live.

The child naturally comes under the dominion of its lusts through ignorance. It feels the disquieting influence of its neglected needs; it feels discontented and unhappy, and therefore it seeks gratification in such direction as experience has taught it it might sometimes be found. He early learns the pleasures of sense. He could not comply with the demands of his physical nature without knowing them; hence, when he feels a demand for something—he does not know what—what more natural than that he should seek sensual gratification. Thus it is according to the figure, that man partakes of the forbidden fruit before his eyes are opened to know good and evil. His first disobedience is in consequence of his ignorance of the nature and requirements of his needs; and, seeking to obtain gratification, he violates the true law of his being. But as man has needs pertaining to his physical, intellectual, moral, and religious natures, and as there are pleasures pertaining to the proper supplying of them, man's lusts may lead him to act in either the physical, intellectual, or moral and religious departments; and, as already remarked, the *grossness* of the lust will depend upon the plan and the means by which it seeks gratification. Reflection will demonstrate that the different lusts, as they are called, differ not in the primary impulse, but differ in the manner of seeking gratification. Man, in the external and finite of his being, may be differently affected by the different modes of gratification which his lust prompts him to seek. Thus the physical effect produced upon him by seeking gratification through his appetite for strong drink, will be different from that produced upon him by seeking gratification through his relish for food or social amusement. Seeking gratification through the improper exercise of any of the faculties of the body or mind tends to produce injury in two ways.

First, the tendency is to call off the attention from the actual needs of the being, so that the proper demands are neglected, and thereby lustful desires become intensified by the influx of an unnatural degree of energy in that false direction. And second, by overtaxing the capacity of those organs which are used for lustful gratification. Thus the inebriate and glutton who make use of their appetites as a means of gratification, often weaken and disease the organs of digestion and assimilation, and thereby disqualify them for performing their proper functions. Man can not engage in lustful exercises without subjecting himself to these twofold evils. And their manifestation will be according to the plane of the lust and the means adopted for its gratification. But while lusts differ thus in their modes of expression, as well as in their primary and secondary effects upon the individual, they are all alike in their inception, and in the end sought to be attained. They all have their beginning in the neglect of some need, which creates a sense of lack, and they all seek self-gratification irrespective of such need; so that all lust, in whatever plane found, is alike in its origin and end. All are fatal to true happiness.

The general sameness of character of all lusts accounts for the singular compounds and apparent incongruities of character found in certain individuals. That is, it is not unfrequent to find individuals remarkable for their zeal in politics, morals, and religion, carried away at times by the grossest lusts. Men, eminent for their piety, sometimes have been notorious for their intemperance and lewdness; and the world have been astonished at it. But a careful attention to the distinction to be made between the true impulse and lust soon solves the mystery. Such men are pre-eminently under the influence of lust in every department of their being—in the moral and religious as well as in the physical. The piety of such men may be ever so deep and earnest, yet its basis is in use. They see nothing in the Divine character or perfections which excites in them love or admiration any further than it is to bear upon their own well-being and happiness. Their love of God is a love of the instrument or means by which they are to become supremely blessed. And their love, after all, is a love of their own happiness, and of God as essential to their happiness. If they should discover that God stood in the way of their future enjoyment, they would like him no better than any other enemy.

Such minds mistake lust for love, and in seeking their own happiness call it seeking God; and in rejoicing in their anticipations, call it rejoicing in God. The man that seeks religion for the sake of securing to himself salvation and endless delight, is just as lustful and selfish as he who seeks gratification in any other way. Man may go a whoring after strange gods as well as after strange women.

Those who appeal to men to get religion in order that they may escape misery and secure happiness, appeal to their lusts, and so far as they influence them by their appeals to their hopes and fears, they stimulate them to lust. The individual who seeks religion for the purpose of saving his soul, is exercising the very impulse which most of all tends to defeat his salvation. Hence said Jesus upon this very point, "Whosoever seeketh to save his life shall lose it," etc. The very impulse is as selfish and undivine as possible. It is for this very reason that the influence of the popular religions of the day is not redemptive in its character. To say to the world that when all should be converted to the religion of these fashionable churches, the millennium would come, would provoke in the highest degree their sense of the ludicrous. Their lustful seeking after self-gratification is so apparent and gross, that they can not even deceive themselves.

It will not be considered a false declaration when I say, that there is no possible resemblance of character or practice between these modern fashionable Christians and Jesus of Nazareth. The redemptive principle of the religion of Jesus can not be found in their religion. The difference is, Jesus was seeking the kingdom of heaven and its righteousness, while they are seeking self-gratification. The impulse in Jesus was that of religious love; theirs is a religious lust. The impulse in Jesus led him to hunger and thirst after righteousness; theirs leads them to hunger and thirst after the things of sense. Jesus, in the things pertaining to the world, was the Lazarus; they are the Dives.

Furthermore, I must be permitted to say that the popular religions of the day are manifestations of man's lustful character, in the moral and religious plane; and that it is more difficult to reform a man in his moral and religious lusts than it is in his animal lusts. It was for this reason that Jesus pronounced his severest woes upon the Scribes and Pharisees, who thought they were righteous and who despised others. Hence he said to them, "Ye shut up the kingdom of heaven against yourselves." Also, "The publicans and harlots do pass into the kingdom of heaven before you."

The proposition reduced to its simplest form is this: True religion can not dwell with lust. "Ye can not serve God and mammon." But the religion of the Pharisee of every age is lust in its highest and most impregnable plane. Hence the more of such proposed religion they have, the farther are they from true religion. Jesus was condemning lust in the moral or charitable plane when he directed that alms should be done in secret. The impulse to charitable deeds which looks to self-gain or self-gratification, brings no reward to the soul of the giver. If he is prompted by a desire after fame, or from a hope of inward satisfaction, he does not act from the true impulse. He who sounds the trumpet in the world or in his soul, to call attention to his charities, can have no reward of his Father in heaven. He who acts from the true divine impulse acts spontaneously, acts as it were involuntarily; that is, he is not aware that he wills. His left hand knows not what his right hand doeth. He meets with a case of need. He stops not to argue the question and determine probabilities and uses. The steel and the flint are in contact, and the spark, comes forth.

In the domestic relation of husband and wife, parent and child, brother and sister, there is much of this moral lust which is mistaken for love. Many professing to be husbands, and really thinking themselves to be so, love the *use* of their wives better than the wife, just as the lustful in religion love the *use* of God better than God.

It is this mistaking *lust* for *love* which begets so many unhappy marriages. The considerations leading to the union are not unfrequently of a lustful character altogether. Thus the young man seeking a wife is constantly trying the question of use. She will administer to his comfort in this way and that, and upon the whole she will be the means of making him very happy. It will not be denied that in a vast majority of cases the man, in seeking a wife, is seeking after his own happiness, and he will cherish her while she conduces to that end. But if he finds himself disappointed—finds that she fails to fulfill his expectation—the ardor of his love begins to abate; and just in proportion as he is disappointed in his expectations will he grow cold and neglectful. So common is this that it has arrested the attention of universal man. The difference between the fondness manifested while yet the newly-wedded pair have met with no disappointments, and that which is manifested a few weeks or months later, has given rise to the expression "*the honey-moon*," meaning that the age of a single moon is usually sufficient to reveal the imperfections of the loving pair, and consequently to cause the ardor of their love to abate. The husband does not find in the wife all that he anticipated. She is not so perfectly adapted to making him happy as he had hoped. Consequently he is disappointed. And as his happiness was the object of his pursuit when he was seeking a wife, and he mistook that lust for self-gratification for love for the wife, being disappointed in his lust, he finds little or nothing of love left.

It is thus, by mistaking lust for love, that so many disappointments take place, and so many unhappy unions are formed; and while the individuals are under this lust for self-gratification, there is little hope of their doing better a second time. It was in reference to this lustful and selfish love that Jesus said unless a man loved him or his doctrines with a better and purer love than that with which he loved wife, children, parents, etc., he could not become his disciple. The simple truth of the expression was, that man's love, or the love of the world, was lustful; and unless man loved God and truth with a purer love than that lustful love, he could not be a true disciple.

The same lustful impulse is found in the parental and fraternal relation. Man is so naturally selfish and lustful, that it is found in every relation, leading him into the broad road to disobedience and sin. And herein is manifested the deep excellence of the morality of Jesus, that it aimed a fatal blow at the lust itself, and thus "laid the axe at the root of the tree." "His fan was in his hand, and he thoroughly purged his floor," "gathering the wheat into the garner, and burning the chaff with unquenchable fire."

In man's social relations the same lust after self-gratification is found. The friendships of the world have this lustful basis, and herein are they distinguished from true friendship. The selfish man or woman seeks social and friendly intercourse for the pleasure or gratification it affords. They cultivate social and friendly relations solely with respect to the pleasures thereof. Consequently their love of *friends* is only in their *use* to them. They love their own gratification supremely, and they love the use of that which will administer thereto—consequently their attachments turn upon the question of gratification. They do nothing, they love nothing in forgetfulness of separate self.

This distinction between true love and lust is to be made in every plane. The true impulse in every plane is the manifestation of the present God in that plane. The obeying that impulse is obeying God. The harmonizing with it is harmonizing with God; and the individual who in all things walks in accordance with its principles is walking with God, and is in the straight and narrow path which leadeth unto life; while he who, on the contrary, is led by his desire after self-gratification, in whatever plane, is in the broad road which leads to antagonism and death. "His lusts, when they conceive, bring forth sin; and sin, when it is finished, bringeth forth death."

There is no middle ground between *love* and *lust*; and unless the distinction be taken where I have taken it, it can not be taken at all. Excuse the principle of seeking after gratification as a true incentive to action, and you have destroyed the distinction between purity and impurity—between truth and falsehood—between holiness and sin. If action in respect to use and the gratification of self be the highest, then, indeed, there is no God—no virtue—no right. Such is the ultimate conclusion of those who know of no higher rule of action than pertains to the sphere of use and gratification. They know of no intrinsic virtue, goodness, purity, etc. They affirm of existence the qualities of good or bad from results. They say that a thing is right or wrong because the result is wrong, and not that the result was wrong because the thing itself was intrinsically bad.

This is a very common error with the world. They are apt to trace the evil in the result and overlook it in the cause. The reason that lustful action is pernicious is not because its results are bad, but because the condition itself is intrinsically false, and can not produce other than false fruit.

We sum up in this. Man will never feel the need of that which he does not lack. He will never feel the need of happiness or gratification so long as every demand of his nature is gratified; because the compliance with every demand of his being will of itself confer all that he can desire, and he will be satisfied. Hence the desire for that which he does not possess demonstrates that there are true and just demands of his being which are not complied with.

Therefore any attempt to satisfy that desire, short of complying with the true demand, will result in begetting false action, which will tend to overtax and disease some part of his organism, creating an unnatural demand in that department, which, instead of bringing satisfaction and content, will bring restlessness and disquiet, calling for still further gratification. Thus lust, when it is conceived, bringeth forth a violation of the normal or healthy condition, which is sin; and that sin in its work, when finished, bringeth forth death.

CHAPTER XII.
MARRIAGE—FREE LOVE.

"Think not that I am come to destroy the law or the prophets.
I am not come to destroy, but to fulfill."—JESUS' *Sermon*.

MAN, as a finite and relational being, is the subject of government. Being produced and developed by laws acting to certain ends, he is the subject of such laws. Being receptive of influences out of himself, he is subject to such external influences, through their action upon his conscious perceptions and affections.

Man, as a conscious being, is the subject of two classes of impulses. One is a sense of affinity, the other of restraint. The first is the natural impulse proceeding from certain relations, and is a spontaneous proceeding from such relation without considering consequences. The other is a reflex impulse proceeding from supposed consequences which will follow certain conditions and actions, and has respect to ends or uses.

This latter class of impulses makes him the subject of outward motions, and bring him under the dominion of laws external to his being. As such he becomes the subject of an external government. As a conscious being, man is the subject of two classes of external government, the one which appeals to his selfish and lustful nature, and the other which appeals to his moral and relational nature—and he is the proper subject of the one or the other government, according to the character of his ruling affection or love.

Man, as a conscious being, can be governed only through some department of his consciousness. That which induces in him volition must address his perceptions, and proceed thence to his affections. For man's affections can not be approached externally except through his perception. This is most manifest to the reflecting mind. Before an individual can love or hate an object, he must be able to perceive it. And his love or hatred thereof will be according to his perceptions. Hence it will be perceived that the individual who is in the ruling love of self, if governed at all as a conscious being, must be governed by an appeal to his selfish nature; that is, by an appeal to his hopes and fears. For so long as he is not under the rule of his moral nature, he can not be governed by its influence. If man is to be controlled, he must be controlled by controlling that which controls him.

The selfish and lustful man is under the dominion of his selfish nature, and whatever controls that nature governs him. And he can be governed, as a lustful being, only by controlling his selfish nature. The same is true in principle of the moral man, or he who is under the dominion of his moral nature. Whatever controls the moral nature governs him; and so long as he is under the dominion of his moral nature he must be so governed. Thus it will be perceived that our proposition is true, that man, as a conscious being, must be governed through that department thereof which rules in him. If it be the selfish, he must be governed by an appeal to selfishness; if it be charity or moral love, then that nature must be appealed to.

Since, then, man must be governed by an appeal to that impulse which rules in him, and since mankind are naturally under the selfish impulse, the first government to which man becomes subject naturally is that of force; and it appeals to his hopes and fears—that is, to his selfish desire for gain or happiness, and his dread of suffering and loss. Hence *selfishness* is the basis of the first dispensation of government. This dispensation of government is not calculated, nor is it designed, to make the comer thereunto perfect. Its end and use is to protect the individual from external or outward evils, and not from that which comes from within. It can not extend beyond the cleansing of the outside of the cup and platter.

The most this kind of government can do is to restrain man from depredating upon the rights of his neighbor, by an appeal to his selfishness. Hence the language of the law pertaining to this kind of government is,"eye for an eye," "tooth for a tooth," "life for life," etc. It does not propose to govern man by appealing to his sense of justice and his love for right. On the contrary its language is, man has no sense of justice or love of right. He is selfish and sensual, and therefore the law appeals to his selfishness and sensualism. It says, Your love of your neighbor is not sufficiently strong to prevent you from injuring him, but your love of self is sufficiently strong to prevent your injuring yourself. Therefore says the law, if you injure your neighbor, we will injure you; if you kill your neighbor, we will kill you; and the same blow which you aim at your neighbor, we will cause to fall upon your own head. In this way this first kind of government takes advantage of man's selfishness to restrain him. It does not cause him to love his neighbor. It does not cause him, from his heart, to respect his neighbor's rights. It does not tend to lesson his selfishness or lust. It does not in any manner tend to make him more true, just, and pure at heart. It only restrains him from giving expression to his selfish and lustful desires.

So far as his motions to action are concerned, he is under the same impulse, whether he keep or break the law. He is as righteous at heart in violating its commandments as in observing its requirements. In either case he is governed by his judgment respecting that which pertains to his self-interest, and in keeping the law he is consulting his own gratification, and in violating it he is doing the same.

So far is this kind of government from tending to make the individual better at heart, that it not unfrequently makes him more selfish by intensifying his selfish feelings. The individual who is restrained from stealing through fear of punishment, and not from a love of justice, is a thief at heart, and will continue so notwithstanding the law says, "Thou shalt not steal," and by its penalties deters him from stealing. His neighbors may thank the law for its protection. But that is the end of its use. It will not improve the *moral* condition of its subject.

Such, then, is the nature and use of this just dispensation, sometimes called the first covenant. It is absolutely indispensable for the protection and preservation of individuals and society. Man left to the unrestrained exercise of his lustful and selfish nature, would not only destroy his neighbor, but he would ultimately destroy himself. And thus the very principle of self-protection compels individuals to associate together under these governmental forms, by means of which the weak are to be protected against the encroachments of the strong, the simple against the machinations of the cunning.

This necessity gives rise to institutions among men which are designed to direct the *manner* of applying this power to the protection of those who institute them. The laws of these institutions are but the expressions of the intellectual and moral character of those who make them. Their wisdom is displayed in adapting the means by which their united force shall be directed to the execution of the governmental will, whether that be just or unjust.

The uses of these external governments are most apparent; by which I mean their uses as a means of protection. The highest possible use of governmental institutions is that of uniting and directing its force to prevent the weak from becoming the prey of the strong, and the simple the dupes of the cunning. If every man or human being had the means of self-protection always at hand, or if none were disposed to encroach upon the rights of others, but were disposed to do good to all rather than evil, then there would be no occasion for governmental institutions. So we see that the uses of institutions, as means of government, have respect to the concentration and direction of force.

But as the selfish man can be governed only by an appeal to his selfish nature, and that must be addressed through the motives of hope and fear, these institutions of government, addressing man's hopes and fears, are indispensable for the well-being of society, and can never be dispensed with until man is elevated to a higher plane, and made the subject of a higher government. In other words, this kind of government must never be taken from man, but man must be elevated above, and thus be taken from the government. There have been two opposite errors respecting this kind of government: one declaring it to be ordained by God, and therefore to be observed and obeyed as an exponent of the Divine will and character; the other holding that all governments of force and blood are contrary to Divine appointment—both of which doctrines are true when viewed in a proper direction, and false when viewed in the opposite one.

In the first place, it is according to Divine appointment that man, as well as every other finite being, shall be governed according to the law of the plane in which he exists and acts; because every thing existing in a finite and relational sphere must become the subject of some law, or it could perform no mission in respect to itself or any other existence. Without law it could not be saved from utter destruction. And being the subject of law, it must be the law of the plane in which it exists and acts; hence whatever may be the law of that plane, it is one of Divine appointment.

Man living in the plane of selfishness and lust must be governed by the laws of that plane; he can be governed by no other. Hence the law of that plane of sensualism requiring "eye for eye," "tooth for tooth," "life for life," etc., is a law of Divine appointment for that plane; and whoever descends into that plane of impulse, and lives there, becomes subject to its law. Having yielded himself servant to obey his selfishness and lust, he has become the subject of its laws. Having taken the sword, he is subject to its use. Having appealed to force, he must be sure to be on the strongest side, or he will be likely to be crushed.

But while the law of selfishness and force is one of Divine appointment, in the sensual plane, it must not be understood as giving law to any other plane. If the law of "eye for eye," "tooth for tooth," etc., was applicable to the dispensation of sensualism, which the Mosaic represents, it does not follow that it is the true law of the Christian or Spiritual dispensation; and he who appeals to such laws of the Mosaic can have the benefit of them by containing under that kind of government. But he must remember, if he wishes to obtain the benefits of the Christian dispensation, he must "put away the old man with his deeds."

Hence, according to the teachings of Jesus, he who would become his disciple must rise above the plane of sensualism. The new law under which he was to come demanded that the law of force should be discontinued. If he would have the benefits of the kingdom of heaven, that is, of the government pertaining to the moral and spiritual plane, he must not resist evil by force; he must not smite back when smitten; he must not indulge in feelings of hatred or unkindness toward any one; he must love his enemies; bless them in the midst of their cursings. He must be pure in heart; he must hunger and thirst after righteousness; he must, in all things, be under the dominion of a love, pure, holy, and unselfish. Such a one would be freed from the law of sin and death; such a one would cease to be a debtor to the law of the first dispensation, and would be born into liberty, not into a liberty to do wrong, but a liberty which had respects to his purified affections.

This will be understood by contrasting the principles of the two dispensations. The first governed by a force external to the subject, constraining him as a selfish being to do things not agreeable to him, thus bringing his will into subjection. The second governed by implanting the true affection within the subject, so that his delight was in the law, according to the inward man. Hence the new kingdom was to be "within." The first was over man with force and fear; the second was to be within man with charity and love.

From this it will be seen, that the first government, or covenant, as it is called, necessarily required external institutions to beget and direct its force to compel obedience to its enactments and edicts. And these institutions were necessarily authoritative; and persons belonging to their plane of administration were compelled to submit to them, as to the authority of God.

The second government or covenant which ignored force, and governed by love, had no use for such institutions, and hence returned the sword to its sheath. Under its administration, swords were to be beaten into plowshares and spears into pruning-hooks. Men were to "call no man master." But it must be noticed that this second government pertained only to those who had come under the rule of charity and love, and thus had put off the old man and his deeds. So long as the individual, in his affections and lusts, continued in bondage to the impulses of his animal nature, he belonged to the first dispensation, and must be continued under tutors and governors until the coming into him of Christ.

Here, then, we see the two classes of errors into which mankind have fallen, the first by supposing that the laws of selfishness and force were applicable to all planes, and that the Christian could find authority under Moses. The second, by supposing that the laws of selfishness and force were to be abolished in every plane, not thinking that such law is just as necessary at one time as another, so long as man continues under that plane of impulse. Herein we can see the wisdom of Jesus in his teachings. He came not to destroy the law, or take it away from man, but his mission was to take man away from the law, and thus to fulfill or consummate the uses of the law. He condemned not the law of force as applicable to those who, in their selfishness and lusts, were under its dominion. And he did not propose to emancipate them by destroying the law. But he did propose to redeem them from under it, by calling them to a higher plane of impulse and action. He proposed to lead them out of Egypt, not take Egypt away from them.

Herein is to be found one of the fundamental errors of Christendom, in not perceiving the true meaning of the *first* and *second* covenants; that is, in not perceiving the true sphere of the Mosaic and Christian governments. Each are of divine appointment in their respective spheres; and neither have respect to time or place of administration, but to condition. The Mosaic, which is a figure representing the governments of force addressed to man as a selfish being, will never be at an end so long as society is in a condition to require that kind of administration. It will not be at an end in the individual until his moral nature is in the ascendant, until he keeps that new commandment of "Love one another." And the Mosaic dispensation will not be at an end in society until the kingdom of heaven is established in the hearts of the members thereof.

The theologian has committed a great error in making the kingdom of heaven a historic affair, supposing that the death of Jesus terminated the first, and introduced the second dispensation, not seeming to understand that the *character* of the government determined to which dispensation it belonged irrespective of time or place. That government which is instituted with respect to, and is administered upon the principles of selfishness and force, is Mosaic, no matter in what age or by whom administered. All civil and ecclesiastical governments which are external and forceful belong to the Mosaic, no matter by what names they may be called. A moment's reflection will demonstrate to a mind of ordinary intelligence and information, that all external human governments are of this character. We have no Christian governments exercising power and compelling external obedience to law. The very supposition is an absurdity. The very moment a government is organized, and clothes itself with external force, its *Christian* character is destroyed.

Christianity, in its true spiritual and saving character, acts only from *within* the *individual*. It is not a government over men or among men. It is a government in man. It cleanses the *inside* of the cup and the platter, and *thence* makes clean the outside. Christians have no need of governments to keep them in the right way. Understand me—*real* Christians, not *professing* ones. They have no uses for institutions, for each obeys the right, and takes upon himself the labor of all needful charities.

Thus it will be found to be a truth of universal applicability, that wherever institutions, and especially legal institutions, are found necessary, the people are not Christians, no matter what creed they profess. Christianity pertains to *character*, not *creed*. External institutions are incompatible with true Christianity. Both can not live and act together in the same individual. Men have been conscious of this, and hence have been involved in doubt and difficulty as to their duties. But there need be no difficulty on this point. Let it be understood, that the man who feels the needs of outward restraint belongs to the Mosaic government, and by it he must be governed; that all men who are under the dominion of their selfish natures have not put on Christ, and hence are under Moses. Such are under the law, and must be continued under "tutors and governors."

External institutions, then, belong to the first dispensation, and will continue to be necessary so long as man continues to live under the dominion of his selfishness and lusts. When he shall be redeemed from such nature in himself, he will be redeemed from bondage to external institutions, and he can not properly be before. The evil, then, is not in the institution, but in that condition of the individual and society which makes the institution necessary; and the remedy is not in destroying the institution, but in elevating man, and thereby dispensing with its need; and until that is done, the law and the prophets must continue.

This brings me directly to the *institution* of Marriage, respecting which so much has been said of late. Like all other *institutions*, it belongs to the external and Mosaic, and looks to the external relations of the parties. Its necessity is based upon the same selfish and lustful principle in man, as is the necessity of all other external institutions.

Its office is *protection*, not *purification*. Hence all its laws look to legal security, but do not attempt to elevate and purify the affections. Those who have written and spoken against the external marriage institution have acted very unphilosophically in supposing that the fault of which they complain was in the institution and not in themselves. I will endeavor to make this apparent.

In the first place, I will do them the justice to say, that the external institution is in character but little, if any, better than they affirm of it; that it is made the means of rendering respectable the grossest lusts; that there is no Christian difference between lust *within* and lust *without* the forms of wedlock; that the individual who looks upon another with a lustful desire, when tried by the standard of Jesus, is an adulterer, whether sustaining the external marital relation or not.

In speaking of the *abuses* of this institution, I would not have them abate their zeal by ceasing to proclaim its infidelity to that inward purity of soul so essential to the true Christian union; but I would have them make a very different use of the fact.

The use which many, and perhaps most of those who oppose the external institution of marriage make of its lustful abuses, is rather to palliate the conduct of those who are lustful outside of its license, by showing that, at heart, they do not differ from those who indulge in the same lustful desires and exercises *under* its licentious permission; thus very naturally taking license, and, when censured by others, pleading the respectable guilt of others as their excuse.

In speaking of the abuses of the marriage institution, I would not plead them in mitigation of lust; nor would I make them the occasion of license. I would refer to them for the purpose of condemning more strongly the foul practice of seeking gratification in that direction.

It is not to be objected to the external institution of marriage that under its sanction the grossest of lusts are practiced in the name of virtue, and that the weightiest evils are the result. Such is not the fault of the institution, but of those who use it for that purpose; and were it not for the institution, under the present lustful condition of society, the same practice would become universal, and would be as respectable as it now is under the sanctions of wedlock. If the external institution does not restrain the exercise of lust between the parties thereof, it does render disreputable its exercise beyond, and thus exerts an influence for good to that extent. It does not make the comer thereunto perfect in his character; but it tends to restrain him in the exercise of his lust toward others, and thus confines its evils to a narrower sphere. One of the greatest moral benefits of the legal institution of marriage is that it tends to restrict the lustful practices of the parties to themselves; and, in reality, this is the bondage of which the objector complains.

The advocate of that which is called "free love" complains that under the legal institution of marriage the parties are prohibited from following their attractions or passional affinities; that although they might have been suited to each other at the time of the union, that circumstances and tastes have changed; that love requires variety, and that in matters of love each ought to be at liberty to follow its leadings. The first great error into which the advocate of free love falls is in mistaking *lust* for *love*. The doctrine that love changes is a fundamental error, and of itself demonstrates that the objector has mistaken *lust* for love. The true impulse known as love has an immutable basis, and will be as constant as the relation and need through which and for which it became manifest.

The nature of *hunger* and *thirst*, as expressive of the needs of the body for food and drink, never changes; and the gratification incident to the proper supply of those needs never changes until abuse and disease have wrought their work. Man's desire for particular kinds of food may change; but that has respect to lustful gratification rather than the supply of a real need.

Remembering our definition of lust to be *a desire for self-gratification*, we shall find that this *change* and *variety* in food and drink looks more to the gratification of desires than to the fulfilling of needs, and therefore belongs to the class of lusts.

True love never changes. From its nature it can not. It being that impulse which indicates an affectional need, it must be as unchanging as the soul and God. Take that known as maternal love, and who that has known a mother's love will say that it demands for its life and continuance variety and change? Tell the mother, as she presses her first-born to her bosom, that she will soon demand change and variety to keep alive her maternal affection, and she would reply in the language of Macduff, "He has no children." No, of all things else, true love will admit of no change, no variety.

In no affectional relation, save that of husband and wife, would the free lover admit that love required change or variety. In the parental, fraternal, filial, and social relations that doctrine does not apply. The parent loves his child, and feels no demand for variety.

What would be thought of that mother who should tire of loving her child, and give as an excuse that her tastes had changed; that once her child was suited to her maternal affection; but that now her maternal love had changed its character and quality, and demanded a corresponding change on the part of the object of its affection? It requires no argument to show that such can never be the requirements of maternal love. The same is true of every other manifestation of the affectional principle. Fraternal, filial, and social love will admit of no change; demand no variety. The brother and sister can love on and love forever; the parent and child can do the same; and true friendship abides in constancy of affection. But *lust* demands variety, and consequently change. When the true impulse is overlooked, and self-gratification becomes the end in pursuit, then comes with it the demand for variety. This is seen in eating and drinking. Hunger and thirst only call for simple food and drink. They will supply the demand. But the moment gratification is consulted, then great must be the change and large the variety. And by far the largest amount of labor and expense is bestowed upon gratification.

The same is seen in the social department. Those who, in their social intercourse, are seeking selfish gratification instead of the happiness and well-being of their associates, are those who demand variety; who themselves are *cloying* of one kind of amusement, and then demanding another. This principle of demanding change in food, in society, in amusement, etc., depends upon that condition known as *cloyed*; and it does not take place in respect to any need. The thirsty soul is never cloyed with drink until it ceases to be thirsty; the hungry soul with food until hunger ceases. But it is not thus with lust; it ceases to enjoy one means of gratification after another, while yet the demand mand for gratification continues. The same principles apply to the marriage relation. True conjugal love never changes. It can never change, because it must rest upon an unchangeable basis. The mode of begetting offspring must be as enduring as the race. The demand, therefore, will be as imperative as the necessity, and hence the desire for offspring must be as deep and fundamental as the soul itself.

The law of procreation demands that in view of the great end to be accomplished, those who unite in the procreative art should unite upon the highest and purest plane. Hence the conjugal affection or love has its basis in this deepest and most immutable necessity of the soul. Understand me—man, in his present condition, is the grand ultimate of all past being and action. And that which took all past ages to accomplish is committed to man in the command to be fruitful and multiply. The future is committed to him. That which comes into conscious being must do so through him, and the true foundation for the fulfillment of the great command is laid in the conjugal union of the male and female souls. To say of the impulse calling for such union, that it demands change and consequent variety, is blasphemously false and absurd. The basis of conjugal love is as deep and immutable as are the foundations of immortality and eternal life.

But let this union be a mere external and lustful one, that is, one looking for self-gratification, and it becomes subject to the law of lust, and consequently, like every other lustful affection, will demand variety. The very nature of lust is to disease and destroy and to defeat the end sought. It therefore brings with itself ultimate cloying and disgust; and to remedy that, it must have change.

That this is the nature of that impulse which *free lovers* mistake for love, is further evident from its associations. The plea they set up is, that every one is free to seek happiness; and consequently when one relation or pursuit fails to conduce to that end, they should be permitted to change the relation or the pursuit, and seek happiness in another. They make the seeking after happiness the great end of life; hence they have adopted very appropriate language, such as "passional attraction," "passional affinity," etc.

For this reason, in their assemblies they aim at self-gratification. Each is striving to beget pleasure. Their assembly-rooms are full of amusements and "innocent recreations," singing, dancing, playing at different games, chatting, etc., all pursued in respect to the pleasures they promise, and not in respect to the good irrespective of the pleasure. The plea is, the people demand cheap amusements, or rather need them. Cheap amusements are the

very things they ought not to have. It is but another name for cheap dissipation. But the advocate for free love complains that the law and public sentiment hold him to his choice, when he has made a bad one. The uses and benefits of the law are seen in this, that they do hold all such to their choice, and by so doing avoid a multiplicity of bad matches.

The individual who is out seeking passional affinities is under the influence of lust, and the sooner he or she is caught and caged the better; such can gain nothing by being permitted to experiment. Until they can rise above their selfish and lustful natures in other things, they will not be very likely to do it in matrimonial affairs.

END.

www.ingramcontent.com/pod-product-compliance
Lightning Source LLC
Chambersburg PA
CBHW081619100526

44590CB00021B/3509